CATHEDRAL
REFLECTIONS

To companions with me on
this second pilgrimage

CATHEDRAL REFLECTIONS

Joan Bristow

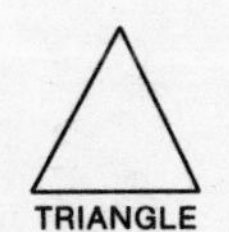

Published in Great Britain in 2000 by
Triangle
Society for Promoting Christian Knowledge
Holy Trinity Church
Marylebone Road
London NW1 4DU

Copyright © Joan Bristow 2000

All rights reserved. No part of this book may be reproduced or transmitted in any form or by any means, electronic or mechanical, including photocopying, recording, or by any information storage and retrieval system, without permission in writing from the publisher.

British Library Cataloguing-in-Publication Data

A catalogue record for this book is available from the British Library

ISBN 0-281-052557-7

Typeset by Pioneer Associates Ltd, Perthshire
Printed in Great Britain by
Caledonian International, Glasgow

CONTENTS

The author and publisher gratefully acknowledge permission to reproduce the following material:

'Here I am, Lord', Daniel L. Schutte. Copyright © Oregon Catholic Press, USA.

'Be still, for the presence of the Lord, the Holy One is here', David J. Evans. Copyright © 1986.
'From heaven You came, helpless babe', Graham Kendrick. Copyright © 1983.
'Jesus lover of my soul', Paul Oakley. Copyright © 1995.
Kingsway's Thankyou Music, UK. Used by permission.

'Shine, Jesus, Shine', Graham Kendrick. Copyright © 1987 Make Way Music, UK. International copyright secured. All rights reserved. Used by permission.

'There is a Redeemer', Melody Green. Copyright © 1982 Birdwing Music/ BMG Songs Inc/Ears to hear music/EMI Christian Music Publishing. Administered by CopyCare, UK.

Permission to use an extract from 'Some Reflections on the Background and Message of Holman Hunt's Picture' given by the Revd Eric Hayden.

Bible quotations are taken from the New International Version, Inclusive Language Edition © 1995, 1996 by the International Bible Society. Used by permission of Hodder & Stoughton Ltd, a member of the Hodder Headline Plc Group. Exceptions are those indicated by 'AV': extracts from the Authorized Version of the Bible (The King James Bible), the rights in which are vested in the Crown, are reproduced by permission of the Crown's Patentee, Cambridge University Press; and 'NEB': extracts from the New English Bible © Oxford University Press and Cambridge University Press 1961, 1970.

PREFACE

When visiting any of our country's national heritage sites, the question will often arise, 'What are we looking for?' Answers may vary from some different styles of architecture to admire or part of our history to learn about, to simply wanting to hear some interesting, even amusing, anecdotes connected with the place. There will be plenty of all that, but an added dimension comes into the picture when that visit is to a place of Christian worship, for a spiritual significance is there to be found – that is, if we are looking for it.

In this second pilgrimage around our Anglican cathedrals in England, I have realized that what makes a difference to our experience is the frame of mind in which we visit. I have found that to be relaxed, not setting a time limit, but allowing myself to simply stand and stare, to sit and meditate, or to return to look at a beautiful artefact is the ideal way for getting the 'feel' of a cathedral. I have to say, also, that I do not make these visits alone, but always choose a companion who lives in the district or who is willing to accompany me. Then together, we share our thoughts, sometimes differing and at other times agreeing. From those shared experiences have come the reflections in this book.

A verse from a psalm sums up the purpose for this follow-up volume to the first book of thoughts from the 22 English cathedrals previously visited: 'Within your temple, O God, we meditate on your unfailing love.'[1] Following on the publication of that first book, I have been asked, on occasion, why I did not include this or that feature in a certain cathedral. The answer is that, usually, there is so much of interest in these houses of God on which to meditate that it is necessary to be selective and simply to include what seemed to speak to me and my companion at the time. As in that book, therefore, I invite readers to find their own special place in the particular cathedral they are visiting, and to let God speak to them there.

Joan Bristow

Introduction

1

LINDISFARNE

Island of pilgrimage

The way to the Holy Island of Lindisfarne is along a three-mile causeway across the Northumbrian sands of the North Sea, when the tide is out, twice every 24 hours and people come in their crowds, by car, coach, or even walking. Pilgrims may, in fact, prefer to walk across the tidal flats of what is known as the Pilgrim's Way, following the markers carefully to avoid the quicksands.

As we start to drive across the causeway in early summer, either side there are massed sea-pinks and other wild flowers. Such a colourful scene would have delighted St Aidan when he trod these sands over 1300 years ago, with the dozen monks he had brought with him from the Christian community on the Isle of Iona off the west coast of Scotland, for they were Celts and love of all aspects of nature was part of their culture. Oswald, the Christian king of Northumbria at that time, had invited them to come to this remote spot. The king had been educated on Iona and was a Christian with a deep faith whose great desire was to see his people evangelized, following a period under the rule of pagan kings.

St Aidan chose to set up his community on Lindisfarne for two reasons. He and his companions would have the seclusion they needed for prayer and meditation when the place became an island at high tide. On the other hand, when the tide was out and they could walk across to the mainland, they had ready access to the people. Lindisfarne was also within easy reach of Bamburgh, where the king was in residence; in fact, we can still see that castle from the island today.

With the renewed interest in Celtic spirituality in recent years, the numbers of visitors have increased, both pilgrims and tourists who are merely curious. But why are we making this trip to an offshore island with no obvious cathedral on it and just the remains of a medieval priory standing beside an even older parish church, when the object of this book is to visit the Anglican cathedrals of England and reflect on their spiritual messages? Simply because it was from Lindisfarne that the message of Christ's love was spread throughout much of England, around the same time as the more well-known Augustine arrived in the south-east of the country to make Canterbury his base. For one of Aidan's first concerns was to start a school where boys could be taught to read and write, and be instructed in the Latin they needed in order to read the gospels and the psalms.

They were trained as priests, but also as missionaries, and once trained many of them travelled throughout northern England, or even farther afield, leading the people to conversion. Women were also trained for monastic life, although they did not travel in the same way as the men. In some of the places visited in this book we shall come across these people educated on Lindisfarne, for in their missionary work they established Christian communities and monasteries which changed only at the time of the dissolution of the monasteries during the reign of Henry VIII. Sadly, a great deal of destruction was done to many of those monasteries in his time, but some of the churches were left and became cathedrals, the seats of the bishops. And, in a sense, Lindisfarne could be called an early cathedral, for Aidan and his successors were bishops.

There are three quite different aspects of Holy Island nowadays. The first is the typically tourist atmosphere. When the tide is out and people have travelled across the causeway, they crowd around the ruined priory, the church, the English Heritage museum, or go a little further – about a mile's walk or short minibus ride – out to the impressive castle, a building begun during the reign of Henry VIII, using stone from the ruined priory, for use as a garrison against the Scots as possible invaders. It later became a private residence, but is now open to the public. The tourists return to wander around the narrow streets to search the souvenir shops for mementoes. By the end of their few hours here they will be able to say, using a popular catch-phrase, 'Been there, done that, got the T-shirt.'

Then, when the tide begins to flow back, they return to the mainland, leaving the small community of residents to get on with their lives, some to shut up shop or restaurant, others to work at their fishing or catering. We watch as cars and coaches leave the car park with their passengers, for we are not going with them, instead we are staying here for a few nights in a guest house.

An easy quietness seems to descend on the island as we make our own way around the streets, then look in at the village hall where, at the time of our visit, there is an exhibition of old photographs of people and events of both recent and earlier years. As we eavesdrop we hear people exclaiming about remembered friends, speaking of memories of events that happened in their schooldays, or looking dreamy-eyed at old wedding pictures. We leave the hall and stroll through the fields, stopping to chat with an elderly resident who, again, talks of the old days but also about today's fishing trade which can be so hazardous in the stormy seas around this part of the coast.

We reach the harbour and walk to the end of the quay from where there is a grand view of both the castle and the priory ruins, as well as the small stone cottages making up the village scene. Lobster and crab pots are piled up around the boats that are pulled up on the shore.

How different would it have looked in those early days of St Aidan's work, we wonder? Certainly the men and boys trained here would also have been encouraged to learn how best to catch fish and to mend nets. And the people here still enjoy the harvest of the sea, as we sample from our meals while staying on the island.

Community was very important to the Celts and, although the population of Holy Island is small, this sense of community is strong, everyone knowing each other. We have now, therefore, experienced two strands of life on Lindisfarne – tourism and community.

Returning to the market square, we stand for several moments looking at the distinctive shape of the Celtic cross in the centre of the square. It is distinctive in that the cross is superimposed on a circle, reminding us that Christ died for the whole world. So we have arrived at the third, and undeniably the most important, aspect of life on this Holy Island – that of pilgrimage.

The following morning, therefore, we set out to trace the Christian story associated with this place, looking through the English Heritage museum as a prelude and being particularly impressed by the lifelike figures of Bishop Eadfrith and his assistant working in the scriptorium on the exquisitely illuminated manuscripts which have become known as the Lindisfarne Gospels, now housed in the British Library. These were copied and painted, it is said, for God and for St Cuthbert after that saint's death at the end of the seventh century. The name of Cuthbert will for ever be associated with Lindisfarne and his story begins on the night when St Aidan died.

Cuthbert was a teenage shepherd boy at the time, guarding his sheep during the night, when he had a vision of angels and of a soul being taken into heaven. He learned, the next morning, of the death of Aidan and at once offered himself at the monastery of Melrose for training as a monk. Many stories of this saint are recorded in numerous books, and here on Lindisfarne, where he eventually became bishop, his spirit lingers.

In the churchyard of the parish church we pause to admire the 11-foot high statue of St Aidan, placed here for a visit by the Queen in 1958. A Celtic cross frames his head, a torch symbolizing the light of the Gospel is held in one hand, and his bishop's crozier in the other. Away in the distance we can see the castle and over to our right the fishing boats in the harbour. This is the man who inspired Cuthbert. The parish church, now dedicated to St Mary the Virgin, is just a few paces away from the ruined priory and is the oldest building on the island, completed in the thirteenth century. We decide to visit it now.

The first thing that attracts us as we enter is the font, with a beautiful modern carving surmounting it, showing a young child holding a bird, symbolizing the Holy Spirit. Near this font, the stained glass window portrays St Aidan, and we cross to the north side of the church to see a corresponding window showing St Cuthbert. We walk down the central aisle towards the glorious three-lancet window behind the altar, where we see our Lord's ascension, his followers gazing up at him as he leaves the earth. The arch dividing the nave from the chancel, we notice, began life as a Norman arch but was later developed in Gothic style. In fact, on our left-hand side (the north side) are three rounded Norman arches, while on our other hand (south) the arches are Gothic.

Briefly we step aside from the sanctuary to the north, into what is known as the fishermen's aisle. Traditionally the island fishermen sit here when they come to church and there is a small altar in this area used for Holy Communion on St Peter's Day. In the window above the altar, Peter is seen with Jesus, as they met for breakfast on the shore after the resurrection. Also standing in this chapel are other indications of fishing – a coracle and a lobster pot.

Back in the chancel we find pleasure in a very small window

showing Jesus talking with the Samaritan he has just healed of leprosy, while the other nine sufferers who had been healed are shown walking off into the distance; the man kneeling at the feet of Jesus is the only one who has bothered to give him thanks. Silently we give thanks for the Christian heritage so well preserved here, then we spend some time admiring something quite special. This is a carpet, embroidered by 18 local women in the style of the carpet page (a decorated page with no writing on it) of St Mark's Gospel in the Lindisfarne Gospels. There are several different styles of decoration, all very intriguing, reminding us of the Celtic knot patterns and the manner in which the strands interweave. We realize how readily the Celts would have taken to the idea of the Trinity, our three-in-one God – Father, Son and Holy Spirit, three strands and yet one Godhead, interacting together in communion.

It was this message of the Holy Trinity that was so important to the early Celtic Christians and which the missionaries took to the pagan people of the north.

- God is great, mighty above all gods. He created the world, all the creatures in it including ourselves, and we can know him as our heavenly Father, loving, caring, protecting and providing for us throughout our lives.
- God is the Son, whom we call Jesus Christ, who revealed the heavenly Father's love by redeeming us through his death on the cross, so reconciling us to God as we repent of all that is wrong in our lives and find forgiveness.
- God is the Holy Spirit, sent by the Father into the world to strengthen us in our Christian living, to help us with our praying, to guide us, convict and challenge us when necessary and to comfort us.
- This is the three-in-one God whose presence we sense here in this holy place, and for whom we make pilgrimage.

This message has proved true throughout the centuries and is one that Christians still proclaim and that still has the power to change lives. What better message on which to base this book of cathedral reflections than that of the Trinity?

Those early Celtic missionaries found no difficulty in explaining such a three-in-one God. St Patrick of Ireland is well known for likening the idea to a shamrock, and others have used the analogy of three joints in a finger, or of frost, snow-flakes and ice, all coming from water. Here in this place we have experienced three aspects of life – tourism, community, pilgrimage – yet all part of a single island.

We leave the church at last and walk across to the priory which, although a ruin since the dissolution of the monasteries in the sixteenth century, still has an unsurpassed beauty. Entering beneath an obviously Norman archway, we gaze up at another distinctive arch known as the Rainbow Arch, set diagonally over where the transept would have been. This priory is not, of course, that in which St Aidan and his monks would have lived; their monastery probably comprised simple beehive-shaped huts made of wood and wattle and the church, dedicated to St Peter, would have been quite small. There would also have been a refectory, kitchen, dormitory, guest house and writing room. Years later, the monks had to flee from the island when Viking raids made it impossible to remain here, and they did so taking the remains of St Cuthbert with them, as he had requested they should do if they ever had to leave. The monks of what became known as The Cuthbert Congregation wandered throughout the north of England with the saint's body for over a hundred years, until they settled in Durham, building that cathedral as his final resting place (see Chapter 22).

It was in 1082 that Benedictine monks came to Lindisfarne, renamed it Holy Island to commemorate the blood shed by the monks of the community during the Viking invasions, and began to rebuild the priory. This new priory was obviously built to resemble Durham, with composite piers alternating with pillars having incised ornament.

There are useful informative plaques dotted around the ruins so it is not difficult to visualize how the medieval buildings would have looked. We leave what would have been the church and inspect these plaques describing the buildings surrounding the cloister garth. The walls have long since crumbled but their remains are sturdy enough, so much so that we rest on one, sitting there gazing across at the ruined priory church. In the foreground some of these crumbled walls are liberally covered with wild flowers, softening the starkness and adding their own beauty. As we sit in quietness, absorbing the atmosphere, the whole medieval scene seems to come alive for us and we can almost hear the chanting of psalms, see the monks going about their more menial tasks, observe them sitting studying Bible passages together.

We are reluctant to move, but there is an even more special place to visit. Following a path beside the wall of the parish church, we descend to a sandy beach from where we can look out to St Cuthbert's Island, a place of less than a quarter of a square acre to which he used to retreat when he wished to be completely alone with God. Just sitting on a bench here listening to the gentle lapping of the waves, once again it almost seems possible to see that saint of old standing waist deep in the water, as was his custom, his arms outstretched in prayer before coming ashore with otters rubbing his feet (as the story goes) and his favourite eider ducks circling around him. We are experiencing something so deep here, a holy stillness that is almost tangible. The tiny isle is surrounded by water, seabirds call overhead and, as we walk along the sand, seaweed and delicate shells are at our feet, as well as what are known as 'St Cuthbert's beads', fossilized remains of a lily-shaped sea creature called a crinoid.

We do not wade out into the water in order to pray, as Cuthbert did, but as we sit here we can offer our prayers to the creator of this beauty, the three-in-one God, for it is his presence we are experiencing, he is here with us as he was with Aidan, Cuthbert and all those who prayed to him here.

PRAYER

Great God, we praise you for your world, created not just for our enjoyment but for our provision.

Lord Jesus Christ, we praise you for your sustaining of this world, and for saving our souls that we might be free to enjoy it.

Holy Spirit, we pray for your strengthening that we might know how to walk in the true way throughout this world.

Amen

We must leave this special spot, go back up the rough track to the church, for it is Trinity Sunday and we are eager to participate in the morning service. We find the church full of worshippers.

There is no bishop now on Lindisfarne, but the Vicar, Canon David Adam, is well known for his Celtic writings. On this Trinity Sunday he says: 'The Trinity is not a doctrine, it is an experience, an experience incomprehensible, mysterious.'

Our pilgrimage around the English cathedrals will be to seek out that mystery and to worship it.

PART I

God the Father

2

WESTMINSTER ABBEY

God Almighty

We were rather reluctant to visit Westminster Abbey for the purpose of including it in this second pilgrimage to Anglican cathedrals in England, but how can we ignore what is one of the most famous and frequently visited churches in Britain, or even the world? It is not, of course, a cathedral in the usual sense of that word, not having a bishop's seat, but is a thirteenth-century Royal Peculiar which comes directly under the Queen's control, and has always had royal connections.

Our main reluctance to visit this well-known building has, however, been because crowds of tourists are usually filling it, making it difficult to find a quiet spot in which to be still and remember our God, for whom it was built. What do all these people come to see? Is it simply an interest in what at first glance might be a museum of monuments and tombs of British monarchs, politicians, statesmen, writers, artists, musicians and other once well-known figures? They will certainly find all of these. Or is it because they have seen pictures or watched television of great state occasions and wish to visit the building where these took place?

One main reason, however, must still be to view the architectural magnificence, so majestic in fact that it almost defies description. We will tour it remembering that, even before this present building existed, Edward the Confessor had established a church on this site, a great abbey used for a life of prayer by a community of Benedictine monks.

Before entering, we pause to look up at ten statues now filling niches that had previously been empty above the great west door. These were unveiled by the Archbishop of Canterbury in 1998 in the presence of Her Majesty the Queen and other dignitaries. The statues are representative of the kind of martyrs known in the 1900s, said to be the bloodiest century in Christian history! So new are they that they seem to glow in their whiteness. They include such well-known figures as Dietrich Bonhoeffer, Martin Luther King, Janani Luwum and Oscar Romero, as well as a lesser-known lady, Esther John. Westminster Abbey is still a place where great people are honoured.

The crowds are enormous today and by late morning there are long queues at the north door, the main entrance for visitors and the official start of the guided tours. It is not, however, a long wait and soon we are inside, our eyes drawn at once to the superb rose window in the opposite south transept. Lowering our gaze we find we are welcomed by both living people, tour guides, and by those long deceased, for immediately great statesmen seem to march forward in their statue form to greet us. They are gigantic and lifelike representations of such people as Disraeli, William Pitt, Palmerston, as well as musicians, among them Henry Purcell who was once organist here. Turning our head briefly we notice another magnificent rose window, this time above the north door through which we have entered. It shows eleven apostles – Judas Iscariot has been omitted.

The going is slow, very slow, as we edge our way into and among the crowd of sightseers. Although we do not fully join in a guided tour, we pause to listen now and then to what is being said and we have, of necessity, to move along with the groups of people. We soon realize that the shrine of Edward the Confessor is considered the most sacred part of the abbey; his burial place is by the high altar although it is not open to visitors. But nearby is what most people want to see, especially those who come from Commonwealth countries: the Coronation Chair. William the Conqueror was crowned here on Christmas Day 1066, and ever since sovereigns have been crowned in Westminster Abbey, including our present Queen.

Turning aside, we move with another part of the crowd into the chapel where Queen Elizabeth I is buried, sharing a tomb with her half-sister Mary I. So crowded is this chapel that we have to proceed even more slowly, and as we do so we look away from the elaborate tomb and raise our eyes to some of the most exquisite vaulting we have seen anywhere. Yet there is more to come for when we reach the Lady Chapel, also known as the Henry VII chapel, for he is buried here with his wife Elizabeth of York, we are even more thrilled by the extraordinary and unusual circular vaulting, with its intricate tracery and magnificent carving. From now on in our tour we are unable to keep our eyes down, but are constantly looking up at the different kinds of ceilings, for they have prompted the thought that the one we worship is high above any monarch, or anyone else we come on pilgrimage to honour, he is God Almighty – El Shaddai.

Many visitors, especially those from overseas, may understandably have reverence for deities from their own cultures. Here we worship the one who is 'God of gods'. As the Psalmist says, he is 'the Lord, for he is good' and we 'Give thanks to the Lord of lords: His love endures for ever.'[1] It is that unique and everlasting love we believe sets him apart from all other gods we might worship. In Old Testament times, in fact, we find Nebuchadnezzar, king of Babylon, sincerely declaring to Daniel, 'Surely your God is the God of gods and the Lord of kings.'[2] Since then we have seen God's love expressed to the utmost in the death of his son on the cross to save the world. Has any other god shown such love?

Leaving the extraordinary Lady Chapel, we proceed around to the extreme east of the abbey into the Royal Air Force Chapel, dedicated to members of the fighter squadrons who were killed in the Battle of Britain in 1940. Here we are impressed by a glorious window, particularly one section where an airman is seen at the foot of the cross, looking up at Christ crucified.

Now we make our way along the south side of the abbey, past a number of chapels commemorating other royal personages. It has been written that such memorials uplift the souls of the living, which is a good enough reason for our pilgrimage, yet the real point of any such visit is to remember the one supreme Being, God Almighty himself, and as we reach the sanctuary where the high altar stands, we pause briefly to acknowledge him. Then we turn into the choir, where the daily services are sung by the 22 choirboys and a dozen lay vicars.

Yet it is not only these daily acts of worship which have made this area so well known, for it is here that so many special ceremonies have taken place.

- Kings and queens have been crowned before this high altar.
- Royal weddings have been solemnized in this place.
- Funerals of famous people, especially royalty, are held here.

Most fresh in people's memories will still be that of Diana, Princess of Wales.
- Special anniversaries and other celebratory occasions have been remembered here.
- National organizations have observed their particular days of commemoration either in this part or elsewhere in the abbey.

Although our great cathedrals, abbeys and other churches were originally built for the glory of God, as places where he could be worshipped in the beauty of holiness, they were also looked upon as focal points where a community, through its various groups and organizations, might have somewhere large enough in which their members could join together in acts of dedication to their particular cause, asking God to bless their work and encouraging other people to support them.

We turn from this, the heart of the church, to walk through what is probably the most popular area of this abbey – Poet's Corner. We tread carefully around memorial stones to poets and writers and glance up at plaques and statues, then turn to stand looking at another statue, this time to one of the great composers, George Frederick Handel. As we do so the music of his famous oratorio, 'The Messiah', begins to sing in our minds, especially the Hallelujah chorus. We can fully appreciate that he must have known a very deep spiritual experience as he wrote this tremendous composition. He expressed his experience thus: 'I did think I did see all Heaven before me – and the great God himself.'[3] Such inspiration has overflowed to countless audiences ever since, as they have felt compelled to stand in reverence while choirs have sung: 'The Lord God Omnipotent reigneth, Hallelujah . . . and He shall reign for ever and ever. King of Kings and Lord of Lords.' Handel's musical inspiration came from the man who selected the scriptures and prepared the libretto, Charles Jennens, who humbly acknowledged, 'The Lord gave the word.'

We pause to look briefly at a small tablet commemorating Henry Francis Lyte, who wrote one of our most loved hymns. The simple inscription quotes the opening words, 'Abide with me'. The great, the mighty God, all powerful though he is, still abides with every individual who trusts in him; surely this adds to his greatness.

Quietly we walk away from this area with its crowds and out into the cloister, remembering this was a special place in the life of those monks so many years ago, for here they wrote and walked; off the cloister was their living accommodation and the hospital. We enter the chapter house where they would have met daily. This is still a beautiful building with one central pillar fanning out at the top. Around the wall is a progressive painting showing scenes from the life of St John the Divine, in particular what he envisaged and wrote about in the book of Revelation. The picture of the last judgement is included, as well as one of Christ in glory. There are also war memorial books here with names of the fallen in them. Some of the windows commemorate royalty.

Eventually we return to finish our walk along the cloister, coming into the nave of the abbey, which is relatively quiet for it is set aside as a place where people can sit and pray. Before we do this, however, we pause to pay homage at the tomb of the Unknown Warrior, as well as the memorial to Winston Churchill. Then we go forward and sink into one of the seats in front of the altar, rather more simple than that of the high altar. The cloth depicts the Alpha and Omega, and we remember that verse in the book of Revelation we have already been thinking about: '"I am the Alpha and the Omega," says the Lord God, "who is, and who was, and who is to come, the Almighty."'[4] There are just a few people here and it is fairly quiet, only a distant hum of chatter and traffic. In this most famous of sacred buildings we have seen so many memorials, yet here we remember the one who is more to be revered than all those others – Jesus Christ, Son of God, and our Saviour. A stillness, in the midst of this busy place, seems to descend and we can pray.

PRAYER

God Almighty, we praise and honour you for your greatness that transcends the greatness of all others, be they royalty, great achievers, or those who have been martyred for your sake.

Lord of Lords, we acknowledge that you are supreme above all that we humans worship, whether that is the materialism of this world or some other god.

Holy Spirit, we thank you that, great as you are, we can know you abide with us at all times and, in fact, that you are here beside us as we bow in this quiet part of this great abbey.

God, the three-in-one, we pray you will remain with us as we leave and go back into the everyday world.
Amen

Having left the abbey, we make our way along several side streets towards St James's Park, but as we do so we are startled as we pass a doorway and what, at first glance, seems to be a bundle of rags and a cardboard box; it is a human being, an elderly woman asleep in the only home she knows. There could be no greater contrast between this and what we have been seeing, yet the stupendous thought remains that the Almighty God we have worshipped stoops down to bless and abide with this sad person. He simply asks that we show the same kind of love for fallen humanity.

3

HEREFORD

Craftsman's art and music's measure

Certain cathedrals are well known for events that take place regularly within them, or for special objects they contain. Hereford has been much publicized for the Three Choirs Festival, which it shares annually with neighbouring cathedrals Worcester and Gloucester, and it is also known as the home of the famous Mappa Mundi, as well as the unusual chained library. Although we are not visiting it at the time of the festival, we have noted a regular lunch-time organ recital which we plan to attend. We arrive early for this, in time to look around the cathedral.

On entering, we are somewhat startled as our attention is held at once by a new and recently installed piece of modern art: a corona hanging at the central tower crossing. This cathedral has changed greatly over the centuries and, ever since the removal of the screen separating nave and choir during the mid 1960s, there has been a more spacious feel to the interior, with the central tower crossing being the focus for all special services. In 1990, therefore, furnishings were added here – a raised pavement, an oak altar table and communion rails. But it was decided that something was still needed to mark its liturgical significance, yet it had to be something that spoke of the joy and hope of the resurrection. Eventually, a young silversmith from Sussex, Simon Beer, was chosen to submit a plan and his idea of a corona that would not only be a decoration but a source of light was accepted. It is not the usual round corona but oval-shaped, and of triple-decked metal chevron links in alternating gold and silver finishes, set with candles, thus making it the symbol of a crown of sovereignty and glory. On our visit, however, the candles are not lit and thus it can readily be seen also as a crown of thorns.

We move down the central aisle and sit near the crossing, quietly contemplating that corona, wondering whether or not it appeals. Later, we ask the opinions of other members of the group with whom we are visiting and the reaction is mixed. Why should that corona be made to look so beautiful and of such costly material? We remember, however, that the cross has been ornamented in many different ways over the past two thousand years, making it into a beautiful symbol when it was, at best, a plain thing, and at worst, a representation of man's utmost cruelty. Yet when we think of what Christ did on that cross we see it transfigured by the light of resurrection and we realize why we now glorify it, why we light it up, why we sometimes even make it jewelled – he died to save us and that means everything to us.

The corona's design of stacked chevron was inspired by the cathedral's wealth of zigzag Romanesque carving, particularly echoing the distinctive decoration around the curve of the Norman arches, and the first impression of the cathedral's interior is, in fact, Norman for the nave was first built in about 1100, but some 250 years later changes were made, with larger windows inserted. A calamity on Easter Monday 1786 caused another significant change. The two towers proved unstable, causing the middle of the building to collapse. James Wyatt, a distinguished architect, was called in to work on the restoration and, as a result, the interior was much lighter, the overall size of the building was reduced and there is now just one tower.

The windows particularly attract us. There is very little early stained glass left in them as much of it was probably destroyed during the Civil War and the time of the Commonwealth in the seventeenth century, but fragments were rescued and used in replaced windows. Others are Victorian glass and tell biblical stories in a beautiful fashion. High up in the north transept aisle are three circular windows displaying musical instruments, with David in central position playing his harp. A window in the north nave aisle shows the life of John the Baptist – even his death is portrayed as Salome carries his severed head on a platter to King Herod. Another window in the north choir aisle has scenes from the life of St Paul, and round in the south-east transept is one with episodes from the life of St Peter.

Four saints are associated with Hereford: Mary the Virgin, Ethelbert, Thomas Cantelupe and John the Baptist. The first place of worship on this site, built more than 1300 years ago, was a primitive shelter of little more than wood and thatch, and it was replaced by a Saxon cathedral of stone, dedicated to St Mary. We are unable, during this visit, to see the thirteenth-century stone and marble tomb of Thomas Cantelupe, reputed to be a wise and caring bishop, nor a statue of John the Baptist, as the north transept is shrouded in plastic sheeting, obviously being prepared for a special exhibition. We are, however, able to look at a statue of St Ethelbert standing on the right of the high altar. This Christian king of East Anglia was murdered near Hereford in 794 on the orders of King Offa of Mercia, but Ethelbert was later considered to be a martyr saint and was canonized. A Victorian floor tile in the choir shows his death.

We find the south transept full of interest. Above an ancient fireplace is a beautiful German triptych showing the adoration of the three wise men when they visited the baby Jesus. On the east wall, opposite and by contrast, we see modern art. Set in three large arches are tapestries designed by John Piper and woven in Namibia. The tapestries depict three trees: the tree of the knowledge of good and evil, with Adam and Eve shown; Christ being taken down from the tree of the cross; and the tree of life, said in the book of Revelation to have leaves for 'the healing of the nations'.[1] We have also passed an interesting display of brasses, and we understand there is a brass rubbing centre, but we do not pause to find this as the time for the organ recital to begin is drawing near. We therefore take our seats near the back of the nave; the young organist is introduced and we relax as the music begins.

The five musical items include pieces by Herbert Howells, J. S. Bach and César Franck, varying in tone and sound to show the full power of an organ that is a magnificent instrument. The more restful harmonies also have a relaxing effect on the mind and spirit so that during the 45-minute recital we are able to just be still and meditate on what we have seen here.

Looking around and remembering the obvious wealth of some of the adornments, we ask ourselves if such extravagance can be justified, in view of so much human need that exists in the world – a reasonable question, and one that has been asked for centuries. We remember, however, that even in the early days people felt the need of a place set apart from the everyday hurly burly of life, to be able to quietly think about the God to whom they have given their allegiance and whom they also want to worship for his goodness in that everyday life. And because of that goodness, and because they realize his greatness, their desire was to make such a place beautiful, filled with the best they could offer. They wish to 'Worship the Lord in the beauty of holiness', as the old hymn says.[2] They believe that such a place is a true witness to their faith and an inspiration. Historically there have been many examples of people wanting to create beautiful objects to glorify God.

- During the years of wandering in the wilderness, Moses encouraged such worship, making a tabernacle in which was placed the Ark containing the Ten Commandments; details of the rich furnishings of the Ark and tabernacle are outlined in an early book of the Bible.[3]
- Many years later, King Solomon built the magnificent temple in Jerusalem, an achievement that led him to humbly ask, 'But will God really dwell on earth? The heavens, even the highest heaven, cannot contain you. How much less this temple I have built!'[4]
- We can still ask Solomon's question as we worship in magnificent cathedrals not only in our country but around the world. Yet those buildings contain some of the world's most luxurious and glorious works of art, mostly contributed to enhance these edifices built for the glory of God.
- As we look up at the great Norman pillars lining the nave, and at the delicate chevron carvings surrounding the curved arches, we think of the masons who worked on them, and those who still preserve and add to the stonework.
- Sitting here we can just catch glimpses of the colourful windows we have admired and we remember not only people of the Victorian era who restored them, but those in earlier years who installed such windows so that illiterate people could learn biblical stories and understand their significance.
- Thinking about the range of artistic work in the south transept, we rejoice that people are still putting biblical teaching into their paintings and tapestries in such memorable ways.
- As we listen to the music, we realize that composers have given their best harmonies and effects; much of it has been heard in the Three Choirs Festival over 250 years.
- Still our eyes are drawn to that corona, a symbol of the torture Jesus went through at the hands of uncaring soldiers, yet also representing how he is now crowned in glory because of the suffering he endured for us and for the world.

Surely this is why everything in our cathedrals is worked with the best of craftsmanship, because of gratitude to God for his love shown in sending his son. There is a desire to glorify him in the very best way we can, either in art, sculpture or musical performance. The organ recital has now come to an end and we applaud the organist for giving such a superb rendering of the pieces, obviously his best.

There are, of course, other well-known items associated with this cathedral that we are eager to see, so we walk along the cloister to a new building at the west end that was opened by Her Majesty the Queen in 1996. Here we find some special treasures. Of prime interest is, of course, the thirteenth-century Mappa Mundi, possibly brought to Hereford to support the cause of the canonization of Thomas Cantelupe. In recent years there was much publicity when the possibility of selling it to fund repairs to the cathedral was being considered, but fortunately generous donations saved it. Nowadays it is only possible to see it through glass in a chamber that is dimly lit in order to preserve it.

This remarkable map was drawn on animal skin and by studying it we can understand, to a certain extent, how thirteenth-century scholars saw the world both spiritually and geographically. At the very centre of the world stands Jerusalem. We try to find the British Isles and eventually see them tucked into the bottom left-hand corner! It is quite a complicated work and time is needed in order to try to decipher it. The map would have been of special interest, at the time it was drawn, to those intending to make a pilgrimage to holy places, and the principal source of the author's information would have been the Bible. The world is shown as a circle surrounded by seas on the map, and seen above this round world is the Day of Judgement with Christ in glory, still displaying the marks of the nails of his crucifixion. This design forms the explanation, the chief message being that Christ crucified is the central fact in the history of the world and that he now reigns supreme in heaven. It is a great reminder of that wonderful Old Testament promise: 'all the ends of the earth will see the salvation of our God'.[5]

In this same building is now housed the chained library, a collection of manuscripts and early printed books on a variety of subjects, including theology, law, medicine, botany and philosophy. The chains were, of course, an early form of security. In more recent years a small chasse, stored in the crypt at Hereford, was discovered to be extremely valuable so that too is now housed in this building. This casket is made of oak and copper plate, overlaid with Limoges enamel and it probably originally held a finger of Thomas Becket. As we view these unique works of art, once again we think of the craftsmanship that went into them and feel full of praise that artists and writers have so often given of their best in the Lord's service.

As there are quite a number of people here, we want to look for a quieter place in which to pray, so we return to the cathedral itself, walking across to the north choir aisle and into the small chantry chapel of Bishop John Stanbury, who was a Carmelite friar in the time of King Henry VI and became Bishop of Hereford. This is a lovely quiet chapel with beautiful fan vaulting and wall carvings, as well as interesting twentieth-century stained glass windows showing scenes from the bishop's life.

PRAYER

Mighty God, we give you praise that when you created humans in your own image, you endowed them with gifts of craft, music, literature, all skills that could be used to give you glory.

Lord, we ask forgiveness that sometimes those skills are only used for our own pleasure and reward, with nothing given for your service; we pray you will also grant us wisdom to know how you would have us use those talents you have given us.

Above all, we pray that by exercising both our artistic gifts, and others that can be used in ministry, we may be able to help other people by enhancing worship, by ministering word and sacrament, or simply by showing compassion in listening when understanding is what is needed.

As we go back into our everyday living, we commit ourselves to you, asking you will use us according to your purposes.

Amen

Looking back at this cathedral after we have left, and as we walk along the banks of the beautiful River Wye beside which it stands, we remember that, because it is so close to the border between England and Wales, it is known as something else: the Cathedral of the Marches. After those early days of Celtic Christianity, this became an area of constant conflict. Yet we rejoice that such a place, built for the worship of God Almighty, has stood here for so many centuries and that people still use their skills to bring fresh interest and beauty that can inspire all who visit.

4

WORCESTER

Creator God

There are two ways of approaching Worcester cathedral and they are in sharp contrast. The most obvious is through busy streets, traffic-jammed roads, much-needed pedestrian crossings, and a complexity of shops. The other, pointed out to us by a local countrywoman in town that day, is a shaded walk beside the River Severn, above which the cathedral towers, and she declares it is 'much the best way'. We take her advice and realize it is the right choice for this is an almost idyllic area, and prepares us well for what we will meditate on in the cathedral.

The banks are lined with trees and the sky today is clear blue with just a few puffy white clouds. Large numbers of swans are crowded together in different parts of the river, mainly beside the banks, while smaller water fowl dart about between them and gulls fly overhead. Pleasure craft pass under the road bridge, taking tourists for boat rides from a nearby landing. The whole scene seems to sing with praise.

Coming from this direction, we reach the south entrance of the cathedral, walk around two sides of the cloister and enter the nave through a door near the cathedral shop. Our eyes are immediately drawn to the striking west window, which incorporates a rose window and dominates the nave. The glorious stained glass is Victorian and was designed by that ubiquitous cathedral restorer, Sir George Gilbert Scott, replacing the glass of the eighteenth century. Stepping back in the nave we look up to examine the colourful pictures clearly showing the biblical story of Creation, as told in the first chapter of the Bible. We can see the scene of God creating animals and the guidebook points us to the creation of vegetation. Such a magnificent presentation of that primal story of Creation prompts an echo within us of the refrain of that Genesis hymn of praise: 'God saw that it was good . . . God saw all that he had made, and it was very good.'[1]

Remembering that this part of our country is associated with the composer Edward Elgar, who was born near Worcester, we turn to look at another superb window in the north side. This is the Elgar window and illustrates his most famous work, 'The Dream of Gerontius', the musical setting of John Henry Newman's poem written in the mid 1800s. It tells of a vision of a just soul leaving the body at death and includes words of what has become a well-known hymn: 'Praise to the Holiest in the height'. Having so enjoyed the walk beside the river as we approached the cathedral and, standing here admiring the west window, it is fitting for us to remember the first verse of that hymn: 'Praise to the Holiest in the height, And in the depth be praise; In all His works most wonderful, Most sure in all His ways.'

Yet as we look back at the detail in that west window we remember this is but the beginning of the biblical story. In the centre lights are shown the early humans, Adam and Eve, first blissfully enjoying the Garden of Eden, but then being expelled from it because they had failed to follow what God had shown them to be the right way to live in that garden.

The Genesis story tells us that God's will was for humans to 'fill the earth and subdue it'[2] and the Psalmist, in a great song of praise for Creation, is amazed that the almighty God who created so much magnificence should be mindful of mere mortals and care for them, as well as making them rulers over the works of his hands and putting everything under their feet.[3]

It seems even more surprising therefore that, from the point when God saw how everything he had made was good and gave humanity all this goodness to enjoy, things later went drastically wrong. Well may Alfred, Lord Tennyson, have called nature 'red in tooth and claw'[4] but humans have much to answer for and, as we look around at the environment in our own time, we have to admit that nature is still far from that glorious ideal set by the creator of it all. God's masterpiece is still being spoilt and not looked after as he requires.

- Rain forests are being destroyed, resulting in whole populations losing their homes and their crops through flooding, because of the lack of trees. Hunger, even starvation, results.
- Fresh air that was once abundant is becoming so polluted by exhaust fumes from cars and other motor vehicles, there are increasing health problems.

- The animals that human beings were allowed to use for food[5] are too often not treated humanely; vegetation is subjected to questionable chemicals, sometimes causing illnesses and creating the need for constant research.
- The proposed development of genetically modified foods is being rushed into without proper thought for its consequences for future generations.
- Wildlife has been exploited in the interests of fashion, to the extent that many species are either already extinct or in danger of extinction.
- Global warming – the greenhouse effect – has become a major anxiety.

We find ourselves questioning, is this the way the creator intended human beings, made 'in his own image', to care for the rest of creation? Perhaps there are no clear-cut answers, but we have to acknowledge that too often it has been economics, greed, selfishness or maybe just plain thoughtlessness that has caused so many problems with our environment. The Celtic Christians knew no such problems for they had such a respect for God's creation, such a close affinity with wildlife that many of those early saints lived in relative harmony with birds and animals. Their stories have a breath of fresh air about them in this age of spoliation of the countryside. We shall find the answer to this wrong way of living at the other end of the cathedral.

Just now, however, we continue our tour of this edifice, admiring what mankind, in the strength given by God, can create from the resources available in the earth. On the way towards the east end we stop to marvel at the nave pulpit carved in British marble and alabaster, showing scenes from the life of Christ, then walk on to stand beneath the tower which was constructed on the foundations of two earlier towers. The nave of this cathedral was rebuilt at the beginning of the fourteenth century and the present tower completed towards the end of it, but a hundred years after the dissolution of the monasteries much of the cathedral was damaged by Parliamentarians. It was restored by the Victorians in the mid 1800s and major restoration work was begun in more recent years.

The rood screen, another of Scott's designs, leading into the choir is admirable in that it replaced an earlier solid stone screen and opened up the view through the full length of the building. Looking up, we admire the choir vault decorated with pleasing paintings, and either side of the choir stalls hangs a banner, one showing St Oswald and the other St Wulstan, the two early saints primarily associated with this cathedral. Stepping aside to the north choir aisle we notice a small oriel window built out from the wall. It originally belonged to the Sacrist's house, which was built outside against the cathedral wall. This security measure enabled an eye to be kept on the shrines in the sanctuary and there are two of these that are of special interest.

In a central position before the high altar stands the elaborate tomb of King John. It seems somewhat incongruous to us that such a tyrannical king, forced eventually to sign the Magna Carta, should lie in this respected place. He is here because of a codicil to his will recording his wish to be buried in this cathedral, for which he had a great love. Another royal personage, but a very different character, lies buried to the side of the high altar. Ornate carvings cover the tomb and chantry chapel of Prince Arthur, the eldest son of Henry VII and brother of Henry VIII. He died at Ludlow when only 15 years old, having just married Catherine of Aragon, and because of his death his brother later became king and also married Catherine. Standing in the chapel and remembering this young prince gives us food for thought. Had Prince Arthur not died at such a young age, what would the subsequent history of England, indeed of the Church, have been?

Turning back to the high altar with its nineteenth-century reredos of exquisite marble carvings showing Christ in Majesty seated between the four evangelists, we are also fascinated by the rather unusual frontal, dating from the late 1960s. This has the full range of colours of the liturgical year, and suggests pinnacles of the cathedral reflected in the river.

Before continuing to the Lady Chapel, we cross to the north side to look into St George's Chapel, which houses regimental colours and other military memorials, including one to G. A. Studdert Kennedy, the famous World War I padre known as 'Woodbine Willie'. Perhaps nowadays he would not have so freely handed out cigarettes to the troops, but in the thinking of his day they brought comfort and no thought was given to the health problems they caused. Of far greater concern was the distress of the trenches and the evils of war. On reaching the Lady Chapel we can see how, when this was built, the result was to make the building of equal length each side of the tower.

Now we can look up at the great east window, which wonderfully brings the biblical story to its main climax. In the west we saw the Old Testament theme of sinful humanity being denied the perfect pleasures of Paradise. Here we see the New Testament solution – the death of Jesus Christ on the cross, paying the price of human failure in order to save the world and bring reconciliation with Almighty God. His life, passion and resurrection are all shown in this meaningful window. As we look down the entire length of the cathedral towards the west end, we feel the greatness of our God and the vastness of his plan, not only in creating the world and placing us in it, but in planning a solution for people's sin – the wickedness seen in the life of kings like John, all the evil that causes wars, as well as our own everyday failings and misdemeanours. The cathedral speaks of the authority of God and the whole expresses his work.

Leaving the east end we make our way towards the crypt, pausing to admire a small sculpture known as the Nottingham alabaster (*c.* 1470), showing Mary nursing the infant Jesus; it is beautiful in its simplicity. From here we descend to the crypt, the loveliest we have seen in any cathedral.

The main exhibition down here is an outline of the history of the cathedral and tells how at the time of King Edgar, in the tenth century, Bishop Oswald founded a Benedictine monastic community at Worcester, building a new church where there had originally been a very primitive seventh-century building when the first bishop, Bosel was installed. After Oswald's canonization soon after his death in 992, his shrine became a place of pilgrimage, but the church was partially destroyed by Danish invaders. About the time of the Norman conquest, a Saxon bishop, Wulstan (or Wulfstan), determined to rebuild the cathedral and parts of his Romanesque building still remain, particularly the crypt. This originally consisted of a central chapel, apsidal at its east end, and rows of stumpy columns (no two alike) which can still be traced.

There is a stillness down here, visitors quietly walking around or sitting meditating. The whole atmosphere speaks of the presence of the Lord, the kind of place where there is a consciousness of prayer having been offered up over hundreds of years. Around the walls are lights set behind a particularly beautiful design known as St Wulstan's cross. This saint was known for his holiness and wisdom, and the earlier founder of the monastery, Oswald, has been called saintly, so perhaps it becomes clear why King John wished to be buried in the place where these two saints ministered.

The exit from the crypt leads us into the south transept from where we can look across to another magnificent window in the north transept, showing the twelve apostles. Here again the colours are superb. Although made in 1866, it does make us think of another of Elgar's works, the oratorio 'The Apostles', telling the story of their work of spreading the good news about Jesus Christ, as outlined in the book of Acts in the Bible. Crossing the nave we make for a small chapel we have previously noted, known as the Jesus Chapel. Here is a beautiful and tranquil place where we can be still and pray.

PRAYER

Creator God, we want to praise you for your creation, yet our words can never convey our feelings for the greatness and stupendous magnificence of nature, let alone our marvel at the delicate details of both large animals and tiny creatures. Forgive us when we spoil or harm flora, fauna, or places of outstanding natural beauty.

Lord Jesus, through whom all things are sustained, as we read in Scripture,[6] we find it difficult to understand the vagaries of nature, violent and freak storms, earthquakes and volcanic eruptions causing devastation, and accept these things will remain a mystery for us while here on earth, but we acknowledge your power and pray for your care and protection of our souls.

Holy Spirit, who hovered over the waters at the beginning of time, bringing light and beauty into a world of darkness and chaos, help us to value more highly what has been freely given us to enjoy.

Triune God, as we recall that we were also created by you, and in your own image, and remembering how you care for us, may we care for the treasures you have given in the nature you continue to create. We would make our own the opening words of the millennium resolution: 'Let there be respect for the Earth . . .'
Amen

Not far from the chapel is the north porch so we leave the cathedral through it, going out into the fume-filled air and noise of traffic. Across the road from the cathedral stands a reminder of what we have seen – a statue to Edward Elgar. How would he, we wonder, feel about the words set to his most popular melody, 'Land of Hope and Glory' these days? Away from the city centre, driving back along country lanes, we can still revel in the glory of the nature God has created – but for how long?

5

CHESTER

God the Heavenly Father

The best entrance into a cathedral is usually by the west door, for this will lead directly into the nave, giving an overall view and the first impression. Entering by one of the transept doors can sometimes spoil that first 'feel' of the cathedral, as we discover when visiting Chester. Coming off the city wall, we walk through the Cheshire Regiment memorial garden which, in the late spring afternoon, is ablaze with multicoloured wallflowers, almost giving an effect of the stained glass we expect to see inside the cathedral, and we pause for a few moments to take in the beauty. Then we enter the first door we see that is open.

Our initial feeling is one of disappointment. The rather sombre style of architecture gives no immediate uplift of spirit, there are few visitors in sight and no lights are switched on so we can barely discern any details. Nor are we able to go into the centre aisle, as this is roped off. We leave, feeling confused.

As we later study the leaflet we have picked up, we realize our mistake. We have entered by the south transept door, in late afternoon, just as Evensong is about to begin in another part of the cathedral, which explains why we saw a notice asking visitors not to walk about. What puzzles us, however, is that the south transept is at least double the size of most transepts so it appears, at first sight, to be the nave, especially as the organ is clearly visible from it. We are to learn that this transept was built to this size to accommodate four chapels, as there was a lack of space on the north side. The small chapels are nowadays used in turn for weekday celebrations of Holy Communion and one of them, dedicated to St Oswald, has a reredos that was carved in Oberammergau.

The following morning we return and follow the path around to the main visitors' entrance, through the exhibition area, into the cloister and then reach the door into the nave. What a difference!

The first sight that greets us is a glorious west window, such as we had looked forward to seeing. One volunteer guide tells us that even when the day is dull, or it is late in the afternoon, the colours seem to shine with light. Designed by T. Carter Shapland in the early 1960s, it is really exquisite and clearly shows some great figures. In the centre is the Holy Family, either side of which are several early saints – Oswald, Aidan, Chad and Wilfrid, as well as the two women associated with Chester. To one side is Queen Ethelfleda, who restored the city in order to defend the area from Norsemen who were settling in the Wirral. At the far end of the other side is St Werburgh, daughter of a Mercian king who became a nun and eventually an abbess. After she died in Staffordshire in the early eighth century, many miracles were reported as having taken place at her tomb. As a protection from the Danes, her relics were brought to Chester where a Christian church is thought to have stood on the site of the present cathedral. This church was enlarged to house the saint's relics and for nearly two hundred years St Werburgh's Minster was a place of pilgrimage. We are to find other references to her as we look around the cathedral.

Although the stonework is rather dark, the clerestory windows give ample light, and what can be seen very clearly on the walls of the north aisle are a series of large and magnificent mosaics created at the end of the nineteenth century by the stained glass artist, J. R. Clayton. Each of the four pictures takes up a whole section of the wall and depicts scenes from the life of an Old Testament character.

To one side of the Abraham mosaic is seen the patriarch preparing to sacrifice his son Isaac,[1] and on the other side he buries his wife Sarah after her death.[2] Next we come to the Moses story, where he is shown holding the tablets of the Ten Commandments. At one side is depicted the well-known episode of his early life when he is discovered by the Egyptian princess as a baby in the reeds by the river Nile.[3] On the other side, we see him seated, with his hands held high by two companions, encouraging the Israelites in their fight against the Amalekites.[4]

The third mosaic shows David as king, holding his harp. The scene beside this reminds us of the earlier story of how he brought the head of Goliath to King Saul, the sling used in killing the giant hanging from his arm.[5] The other picture here is a sad one: David is seen mourning the death of his son Absalom.[6] Finally we see Elijah on top of Mount Carmel,[7] while another scene is of him being woken up by an angel who has brought him provisions,[8] and on the other side he confronts the sinful King Ahab.

As we look at each of these mosaics we remember the care and protection of God for his people, the kind of attributes we would expect from an earthly father, but perfectly expressed in our Heavenly Father.

- Abraham was put to the test on several occasions during his life, and at times he must have been puzzled about the God he had felt had called him to leave his home country and venture out into a strange land. He learned, however, that it was only in obedience to this God that he could experience the guidance, strength and provision he needed.
- Moses must have been conscious that God had overruled in his life, ordering events, protecting him, equipping him for the tremendous task he had ordained for him, and even when things seemed to be going terribly wrong, because of the impatience of the people he was leading, still he looked to God to know what to do.
- David had learned the goodness of God, as we realize in reading the Psalms. Throughout his life, David had sung to the Lord and one of his songs, 'The Lord is my Shepherd'[9] is still among the most-loved ways of praising the Lord. Yet he was to learn something even deeper after he had sinned badly by committing adultery and murder, for he was to experience God's complete forgiveness as soon as he repented. 'As a father has compassion on his children, so the Lord has compassion on those who fear him; for he knows how we are formed, he remembers that we are dust.'[10]
- Elijah was dedicated to God, striving to bring the people of Israel to a full commitment and to abandon false gods and idols, but he was frustrated because of a weak king with a wicked wife (Jezebel). In the great contest on Mount Carmel, he experienced the result of utter trust in the God he served.
- All these attributes of God, learned by people who lived so long ago, made it so right for them, and for us still, to address him as Heavenly Father. This is how Jesus taught us to pray, and

this is how he himself looked to God during his earthly life.
- Above all, we know that not only is God a father to obey, to trust, to be forgiven by and to be dedicated to, but one who provides, protects and guides. He is the God who is Love, in all that means, love that is concerned for each one of us individually, as well as for the world as a whole.

Glancing back at that west window, we are sure this is what those saints portrayed there knew so well.

Turning from these meaningful reminders of the way in which the people whose stories are told in the Old Testament knew God as everything that a loving father should be, but so much more, we make our way to the oldest part of the present building, the north transept. It was after the Norman Conquest that the second Earl of Chester, Hugh Lupus, decided the minster should be transformed into a Benedictine abbey. Having as a friend none other than Anselm, who was later to be Archbishop of Canterbury, he wisely sought his help and Anselm arrived in Chester in 1092 with some of his own monks. So the abbey came into being, although it took about 150 years to rebuild the Saxon minster and replace it with a Norman abbey. Just a few parts of this Norman abbey can still be seen in the north-west corner of the nave today. The church was rebuilt again during the mid thirteenth century, this time the process taking 250 years, but no sooner had it been completed than the monasteries were dissolved by Henry VIII, although almost immediately the diocese of Chester was created and the abbey became the cathedral we know today. It went through a restoration process in the nineteenth century, and there have, of course, continued to be additions of works of art.

One of these additions is found in a small niche in the wall here in the north transept. This is a cobweb picture, showing Mary with the infant Jesus, delicately painted on the net of a caterpillar. It comes from the Austrian Tyrol and was painted by the nineteenth-century Tyrolean artist Johann Burgman, as a copy of a picture by a medieval artist in a church in Innsbruck.

Being midday by now, we walk along to the refectory for a light lunch. This was the monks' dining hall and as we eat we try to imagine ourselves sitting where they once sat, listening as they would have done to a reading by a monk standing in the canopied wall pulpit, still to be seen high up on the south wall. We rather wish one of the clergy would do that today, but none comes so we finish our meal and return to the main part of the cathedral.

The wooden rood screen showing Jesus on the cross was designed by Sir George Gilbert Scott. There is, in fact, much fine carving in Baltic oak in the choir, from the intricate pattern behind the rood screen to the canopies (originally designed to shelter the monks from the cold draughts whistling down from unglazed windows above) to the misericords and bench ends. One particularly attractive carving, in front of the Dean's stall, dates from the fourteenth century and shows the Chester pilgrim, complete with large hat and stick in hand.

Walking through to the Lady Chapel we find, near the entrance, an early fourteenth-century shrine which once contained the relics of St Werburgh. It would be here that pilgrims came to pray for help and healing, but the bones of the saint were probably removed and the shrine defaced when the monasteries were dissolved. It was, however, later reconstructed and a figure of the saint was carved, in the early 1990s by Joseph Pyrz, to stand in the upper part. We feel almost a hush as we stand here, for this king's daughter is said to have been humble and obedient, given to prayer, and so committed to Christ and the Church that she refused marriage, choosing instead to enter an abbey. It is good to remember her this way, rather than by the legend of her restoring a goose to life, although the sign of the goose was adopted in the Middle Ages as proof of having taken a pilgrimage to this shrine, and the motif can still be seen around the cathedral nowadays.

It seems most natural, because of her prayerful life, to turn towards the north aisle and into the small chapel dedicated to the saint. The beautiful stained glass window above the altar has at its centre the nativity scene of Jesus. This is a special place set aside for prayer.

PRAYER

Heavenly Father, humbly we bow here and pray we may be counted as worthy to be called your sons and daughters, thanking you for your love which provides, protects, guides and forgives.

Lord Jesus, thank you for teaching us to speak to God in prayer as our Father, and for showing us by your example how to relate to him in our daily living.

Holy Spirit, we remember how Our Lord said that God is Spirit and we should worship him in spirit and in truth.[11] *Help us to pray in the right spirit at all times.*

Three-in-one God, when we do not thoroughly understand your ways with us, help us to simply trust and wait for the fulfilment of your will in our lives.

Amen

Back in the cloister we walk out into the garden, which was once the centre of the monks' domestic life, and find there one of the modern sculptures added during the 1990s. This is by Stephen Broadbent and is called, 'The Water of Life', being a portrayal of the meeting of Jesus with the Samaritan woman at the well in Sychar. Jesus is shown seated, while the woman bends over him with a bowl, and the text around the base quotes: 'The water that I shall give him will be an inner spring always welling up for eternal life.'[12]

The portrayal is so unusual we need to stand and contemplate it, and when we do we find different kinds of thoughts filling our minds. Remembering how we first entered this cathedral last evening, and how mistaken we were in our initial impressions, we remember too how those Old Testament characters were often mistaken in their ideas about God, until they thought more deeply. This woman depicted here also seemed naïve at first, until she realized just who Jesus was. The message clearly is that we need to ponder the spiritual messages in these cathedrals, rather than dismissing what is not at first understandable to us.

6

GLOUCESTER

To question God?

Tourism means different things for different people, but for many it has almost become synonymous with visiting old buildings and ancient sites of national heritage, and most tour companies include such places in their itineraries. A nostalgic fascination with the past seems to be part of life's interests, anything from valuable antiques to archaeological finds. We want to know about works of art and craftsmanship, we are keen to be told how people lived centuries ago, what led to their development and to understand more deeply the kind of faith they had. The life of the medieval monks holds a special appeal, and we catch glimpses of this in our visits to various cathedrals, none more so than in Gloucester, for here it can be envisaged as clearly as in almost any other place in our country.

Over 1300 years ago, a small Anglo-Saxon monastery was founded here by Osric, a prince of Mercia, but during the eleventh century it was given to Benedictine monks. By the time of the Norman conquest, however, there were only two monks and eight novices left but, as Gloucester was such a strategic place commanding the ford of the River Severn, William the Conqueror determined to revive the monastery. He appointed his friend and chaplain Serlo, who had been trained at Mont St Michel in Normandy, first abbot of the new foundation, named St Peter's Abbey. By the time of Serlo's death, after 33 years, there were 100 monks in the monastery, he had rebuilt the monastic buildings and had begun a new abbey church, a great deal of which is still standing. Some rebuilding work was carried out during the fourteenth century and some new building in the following century. At the dissolution of the monasteries by Henry VIII the abbey church became Gloucester Cathedral. There were major repairs and alterations in the 1700s and in Victorian times extensive restoration.

Evidence of much of this history is seen as soon as we enter the nave and we marvel at the enormous solid Norman pillars, the relatively plain Early English vault and the huge fifteenth-century west window that now contains Victorian glass. The brilliance of the colours of this window impress us with its scenes from both Old and New Testaments, the nativity of Jesus shown in one central panel, while he stands in risen glory above. Glancing at the aisle windows, we note how several depict his ministry of healing and teaching, as well as the crucifixion and resurrection.

English history is portrayed in other windows, one showing the coronation of the boy king, Henry III, which took place here in 1216, the only English king to have been crowned outside Westminster since the Norman conquest, another picturing the burial in this cathedral of Edward II in 1327, after his murder at Berkley Castle. Edward's funeral was carried out with great pomp and ceremony and, as a result, pilgrims began to flock here to pay homage at his elaborate tomb, erected by order of his son, Edward III.

Although it would be here in the church that the medieval monks spent regular times of worship, this would have been only part of their daily living, so we turn aside now to remember how they spent the rest of their time. Moving across to the north side of the nave we go through a door into the cloister and as soon as we see it we stop abruptly, gasping at the sheer beauty and contrast of the vaults here and in the nave. Having become accustomed to seeing beautiful vaulting in naves and chapels, we are dumbfounded to see such glorious work in the place where the monks had their living quarters. We are in the part called the Great Cloister and, in a word, it is fantastic! The fan-vaulting has been likened to an avenue of trees with their branches meeting overhead, and that is not a bad description. It dates from the fourteenth century and apparently was later copied for Henry VII's chapel at Westminster Abbey, as well as in other places.

It was here that the monks could go from one part of the monastery to another sheltered from the weather, but it was also an enclosed area where silence was strictly observed. Here they could be quiet for meditation, reading and writing in the twenty carrels (study recesses) along the south walk, and each carrel would be fitted with a wooden desk at which a monk would sit. We turn a corner into the east walk which, in medieval times, would have been a slype (passage) leading out to the monks' burial ground. This part would also sometimes have served as a locutorium where the rule of silence could be temporarily lifted and the monks would be allowed to speak to each other. Just here also the chapter house is situated where, every morning, the whole community would meet to discuss abbey business, to discipline brothers who had erred, to allocate work for the day and to listen to a chapter of the Rule of St Benedict. The monks' dorter (dormitory) also led up from this section of the cloister and beneath it would have been the warming-room and reredorter (lavatory block). At the far end of this east walk we see a door that would have led to the infirmary.

The most interesting part of the cloister is, however, along the north walk where we come to a lavatorium. This was the monks' communal washing area, a long stone basin with holes at regular intervals for drainage. We stand here amazed again, for never was there such a beautiful washroom! Overhead is a glorious diminutive fan-vault, and nowadays the windows have stained glass pictures all associated with Jesus's earthly life and all of which, appropriately, are connected with water, such as Jesus walking on the waves and seated in Simon Peter's fishing boat with a great catch of fish. Here the monks would wash their hands before a meal, drying them on towels hanging in a recess opposite, for the Rule of St Benedict placed great emphasis on cleanliness. Then they would line up in a double row at the refectory door to await the senior monk, who would preside at dinner.

As we continue our walk around the four sides of the cloister we feel a deep sense of history, especially as we return along the north side to reach the door near the north transept of the cathedral through which the monks would have passed after coming from their dormitory for the night watch office of Vigils. Regularly throughout the day they would return for the other monastic 'Hours' and for high mass.

In those early days a great screen separated the nave from the choir, the choir being reserved for the monks and the nave for the townspeople to come and listen. A less ornate screen replaced an earlier one during the early 1800s, and the choir itself was refurbished by Sir George Gilbert Scott later that century. Having entered the choir, we stand looking down at the floor, admiring a set of sgraffiti tiles depicting Old Testament scenes, from Adam and Eve in the Garden of Eden to the building of the Temple by King

Solomon. Then we turn our eyes upwards towards the elaborate lierne vault of the choir above the high altar. Central among the many decorative bosses is one of Christ in glory, surrounded by others of angels with different musical instruments.

Having glimpsed something quite different we leave this area to take a closer look. This is the south east ambulatory chapel, where new glass by Thomas Denny was installed in 1993. The window so impresses us that we sit here for several moments deciphering the picture, which is mainly in blue glass. It shows the apostle Thomas confronting the risen Christ in the centre panel, and we meditate on the story as we look at it. Doubting Thomas, as he has been known ever since he refused to believe that Jesus had risen, when the other disciples told him they had seen the Lord, saying he would not believe unless he could put his hand in the wounds Jesus had suffered when he was crucified three days earlier.[1] Then just a week later, when Thomas and his friends were together in the upper room, Jesus appeared to them again and held out his hands to Thomas inviting him to touch them. So the doubting disciple became the believing one. It is such a pity this disciple has always been known for his doubting, for another apt description of him would be 'questioning', as this is how he appears in other parts of the gospel story, and really he was simply doing what most young Jewish men of his day would do. We remember how, in the 'seder' service at Passover, four questions were traditionally asked by the youngest child. It would therefore be natural for Thomas to question, and Jesus answers him in the most loving manner.

Still, today, people question, voicing their doubts and that can be no bad thing for in this way they confront their faith and learn. We wonder, did those medieval monks of old have times of doubting, longing to question and find clear answers? In those regular times of worship, when they chanted the psalms, how did they relate to some of the words? The whole Psalter was, in fact, at the centre of the Church's daily prayer and the monks would have read it through regularly, perhaps every week, but in any case covering all 150 psalms over a month. They would have come to realize what a unique and wonderful book the Psalter is, where there is always a psalm that fits whatever mood they happened to be in, be it rejoicing, sorrowing or questioning. As they sang or recited the words, there would be answers that would relate to the way they felt about why innocent people suffer, why ungodly people seem to prosper, why at times God does not seem to answer prayer and why he feels so far away. They would even be able to find words that expressed their feelings of anger. If God is such a loving Heavenly Father, why was there so much suffering in the world?

- In fits of depression, words like, 'Why, O Lord, do you reject me and hide your face from me?'[2] would be so meaningful. But then, would they remember how Jesus, when he was dying on the cross, cried out the words at the beginning of another psalm, 'My God, my God, why have you forsaken me?'[3] Surely this would help them to take heart; rather than to turn away from God, just call on him in prayer.
- When confused, wondering what they should do in a given situation, would not the words, 'How long must I wrestle with my thoughts?' express their feelings, and by the end of the psalm hopefully they could be more positive, saying, 'But I trust in your unfailing love.'[4]
- Whatever the cry of the Psalmist, always those monks would be led on and out of their despair. They would know that as they sang, 'Hear my prayer, O Lord, listen to my cry for help; be not deaf to my weeping'[5] they could continue on to the next psalm, with the words, 'I waited patiently for the Lord; he turned to me and heard my cry . . . he put a new song in my mouth, a hymn of praise to our God.'[6]
- Looking away from themselves and at the troubles in the world outside the confines of the monastery, did they ask, 'Why do the wicked revile God? Why do they say to themselves, "He won't call us to account"?' The answer near the end of the same psalm would lift their spirits: 'The Lord is King for ever and ever . . . You hear, O Lord, the desire of the afflicted; you encourage them, and you listen to their cry.'[7]
- As they praised God for the wonders of his creation, still they might question – how could such a mighty God be concerned with so much detail; even more, why should he bother with people and nations, to which they would be able to reply: 'Blessed is the nation whose God is the Lord . . . From heaven the Lord looks down and sees all humanity.'[8]

In the side panel of the window we see symbols of nature, as well as items of Cotswold crafts. A volunteer guide points out that Psalm 148 is depicted here, and, yes, we can see great sea creatures, lightning and hail, snow and clouds, the effects of stormy winds, mountains and hills. So, with the Psalmist, a hymn of praise wells up in our hearts: 'Praise the Lord . . . for his name alone is exalted; his splendour is above the earth and the heavens.'[9]

Returning to thoughts about Thomas, we remember that when he came face to face with the risen Christ he realized that, whereas until that time he had thought of him simply as a man, now he recognized someone far greater. So he exclaimed: 'My Lord and my God!' He realized that, were he to turn away from the truth of the resurrection, there might well be greater doubts, imponderables, unanswered questions. He might not be able to understand everything, but all he was being called upon to do was to believe, as people have been urged to do ever since. From statistics, we know that a large percentage of people in our country do believe in the existence of God; it is Jesus, as Son of God that so many question. True, this seems a mystery to people of other faiths, or of none, and a mystery that cannot be fully answered in this life. But for those who believe, they know it is true because of the difference his presence makes to their lives.

At last we leave this chapel to take a look at one or two other details, although there is so much of interest in this cathedral we could spend hours here. From this point we can look up at the great east window, erected about 1350 to commemorate the local knights and barons who fought with Edward III and the Black Prince at the battle of Crécy and the siege of Calais in the mid-fourteenth century. Then we walk on to the south transept to see something unique. High up at one side is a stone bracket known as the Prentice Bracket, thought to be a memorial to an apprentice who may have fallen to his death from the vault above. It is L-shaped, like a medieval equivalent of the architect's T-square, and shows the master mason and the apprentice. A sad tale, for obviously the master is trying to save his young assistant.

At this point a volunteer guide kindly unlocks a door and leads us down into the crypt. This is usually kept locked because it is difficult to walk around, being dark and dank, but it is tremendously fascinating. Our guide points out five altars which correspond to five in the cathedral above. In medieval times, there would also have been five more in a gallery overlooking the choir and presbytery, all of which would have been in daily use. He shows us squat pillars, explaining how reinforcement was needed to take the full weight of the choir above. Now we really do feel we have stepped back into medieval history!

Returning to the main part of the cathedral, we walk to the far east end and into the Lady Chapel, the last major building work of the abbey, probably dating back as early as 1483. Unusually, there are chantry chapels either side with singing galleries above, and the glass in the tracery of the chantry chapels is medieval. The reredos was badly damaged over the centuries but in recent years three beautiful embroideries have been placed against it in the three principal niches, portraying the Nativity, the Annunciation and the visit of the shepherds to the manger. They remind us of the Virgin Mary and the questions that would have been in her mind when told that she was to give birth to a baby who would be called the 'Son of the Most High'[10] and the feeling of puzzlement that shepherds should come to worship the baby. She could simply remember these amazing happenings and ponder on them in her heart.[11] Which is what we will do as we pray.

PRAYER

Lord God, as we ponder about the state of the world and the way in which, in so many places, there is fighting and violence, we find ourselves asking, Why? Why do you allow such things to happen? Why do you not stop evil people before they inflict so much suffering on innocents? When we cannot find answers to such questions, we pray you will speak peace to our hearts and reassurance that you are indeed always in control.

Jesus, Saviour and Lord, we praise you, even though we may be in tears as we do so, when we remember how you died on the cross to save the world from its sin. Humbly we thank you because that salvation included us as individuals.

Holy Spirit, grant us strength to cope with our moods of depression, ability to rise above sorrows and perplexities, and simply to trust.

God of Trinity, we pray we may learn how to praise you, even when we do not fully understand what is happening in our lives.

Teach us that we do not need to understand every small detail, or the full extent of theology, to follow you and be known as a Christian. Strengthen our faith, we pray.
Amen

Leaving the chapel we return to the cloister, then walk out into the cloister garth. From this aspect we can look up at the great 225-foot tower with its pinnacled coronet, something that makes this cathedral visible from miles around and one that is frequently pointed out by coach drivers as they bring tourists to this beautiful part of the country.

We may not have answered all the questions in our minds which rise from the daily news fed to us by the media, but we feel a deep certainty about God. As one hymn-writer has said, 'I cannot tell why He, whom angels worship, Should set His love upon the sons of men . . . But this I know, He heals the broken-hearted, And stays our sin, and calms our lurking fear.'[12] So many things we cannot begin to understand; we can but concentrate on what we know – God's promise of love and care is sound and true.

7

WELLS

God of time and eternity

Our coach driver has given us five hours to spend in Wells before he returns for us so we consider this to be ample time for a leisurely visit to the cathedral, as well as taking a look at adjoining places of interest. This could be so in some cathedral cities, but not in Wells! There is so much here to explore and enjoy that, we are to discover, there is never long enough and time seems to fly as we look, admire and drink in the atmosphere.

Wells is a city that was mentioned in the Domesday Book and called then Welle, a word meaning 'the Spring' and there are three springs close to the bishop's palace which may have been associated with some kind of pre-Christian shrine. Later evidence of chapels and a great Saxon minster church has, however, been revealed in the past two centuries. This church, dedicated to St Andrew, was founded in 705 by Bishop Aldhelm, probably under the patronage of King Ina of Wessex. The Diocese of Wells, created in 909, was later moved to Bath, although in the thirteenth century Wells became a cathedral again, this time for the Diocese of Bath and Wells. By then there was a new building on a fresh site north of the old cathedral and it is the one still standing today.

Although there is no grand entrance from the city to the cathedral, the approach being by a narrow gate, once through that gate the view of the west front is truly spectacular, even though many of the original 400 statues were destroyed in the seventeenth century at the time of the Civil War and Monmouth's Rebellion. There are, however, enough for us to admire of kings, knights, angels, saints, prophets, apostles and, high over all, the risen Lord Jesus Christ. Biblical scenes from both Old and New Testaments are there in plenty. All were at one time painted and gilded but that kind of decoration has long since been removed.

Splendid as this west front is, we are still not prepared for the magnificent interior. We have first visited the cathedral restaurant and shop, so have entered from the cloister and now find ourselves looking down the full length of the nave. The initial sight takes our breath away, yet it is more than just the wonder and beauty of the architecture that so affects us. We are filled with a sense of awe as we look right through that nave and up to the rood, with the figure of Jesus hanging high up on the cross, the sunlight shining through the windows lighting up that crucial symbol, while the figures of Mary and the apostle John either side are slightly in the shadows. It is a familiar scene highlighted in a number of churches and cathedrals, and in some places it seems stark and gloomy but here, although it is such a cruel scene, it seems to convey a different feeling. Perhaps the very light and slightly golden-coloured stonework has something to do with it but as we rest on a seat we feel the need to just silently gaze, worshipping our God who so loved the world that he sent his Son to die in this way. And maybe the brilliance that now seems to shine out of that scene is because we are privileged to understand and appreciate all that his death means for each one of us.

Yet there is something else that makes the familiar scene so much more impressive here than elsewhere. That is the series of great arches beneath it which seem, so to speak, to be lifting Jesus as high as possible for all to see. These arches are a very special feature of this cathedral and are known as scissor-arches, their shape making the name obvious. Apparently the central tower was originally planned to be lower but extra height was added, as well as a wooden, lead-covered spire. The added height and weight made the foundations sink on one side, which could have meant a collapse of the tower. A solution was thought up during the fourteenth century by William Joy, a master mason, who constructed the scissor-arches on three sides of the crossing, beneath the tower, and these distributed the stresses and braced the tower, thus stabilizing it ever since. The spire later burned down and was never rebuilt.

The addition of these arches has given this great edifice a unique kind of splendour. Later, as we walk around and stand first in the north transept and then cross to the south transept, we shall see the effect those shaped arches have from different angles. In the transepts the crucifixion scene cannot be seen; instead the arches simply lift our spirits in praise to our God.

While still at the west end, however, and looking down the full length of the nave, we also admire the delicately painted ceiling patterns and ribbed vaulting. When the present building was planned, the idea was that it should be entirely English 'Gothic', the earliest of its kind.

An organ has been in place above the entrance to the choir since the mid fourteenth century, although the present instrument is mid Victorian, rebuilt a couple of times since. Just now it is being played softly and we recognize one of our modern songs: 'Be still, for the presence of the Lord, the Holy One is here.' (David J. Evans)[1] As we walk through the nave and pause to look into one of the chantry chapels, we bow our heads briefly for the words are so fitting.

By the fourteenth century, it seems there were so many services being held at the different altars in the cathedral that precise time-keeping became essential. Special clocks were therefore installed, one inside and the other on the exterior wall, both operated by the same mechanism although the outdoor clock was made about 80 years after the interior one. These clocks have become such a well-known feature at Wells that visitors often make them their initial point of interest. As it is nearly 2 pm we also deliberately turn from other details and make our way to the north transept to watch the chiming, joining several other people already seated and waiting. Just before the hour a priest calls us all to a brief prayer and gives a blessing. Then the small figure high up and to one side of the clock, known as Jack Blandiver, strikes the bell in front of him. A quarter-hour later, and at each quarter, he kicks two bells with his heels while his head jerks from side to side. What really attracts attention, of course, are the puppet figures of knights on horseback, above the clock-face, who ride round and round as if in a tournament every hour, with one of them being unceremoniously knocked off his horse regularly. When the striking is over we walk closer to the clock and read what is said about this, namely that the same knight has been knocked down every hour for over six hundred years!

This fourteenth-century clock is the second oldest still in working order in Britain. An even older mechanism can be seen in Salisbury although without a clock-face. The face on the Wells clock, however, is both fascinating and beautiful. It is a 24-hour clock, not digital of course in the modern sense, but circular with a clock-face showing midnight at the bottom and noon at the top. A large sun in the outer circle points to the hour and a small star in an inner circle to the minutes. A third circle shows the day of the lunar month and right in the centre a disc gives the phases of the moon.

For all the fascination this remarkable clock brings, however, it is something more meaningful and impressive that has been added in recent years which captures our attention. Immediately below the clock is an exquisitely carved figure of Christ rising from the dead. From his outstretched arms the bandages are shown unravelling and the indication is that the body shroud will also soon be off, to be laid aside in the tomb. Carved in yew wood by E. J. Clack during the 1950s, it was surely an inspiration to put such a statue here, emphasizing the absolute control of our God over time.

The well-known passage from the biblical book of Ecclesiastes comes to mind, verses that were turned into a modern song not too many years ago. The biblical words begin by reminding us that, 'There is a time for everything, and a season for every activity under heaven.'[2] Yes, indeed, throughout human history we can see how God chooses a right time for his purposes.

- Although we read of millions, even billions, of years ago, God chose a certain time for the creation of our world as we know it, developing it – according to the first chapter of the Bible – in six stages (what the Bible calls 'days'), with time for rest at the seventh stage.
- What is so striking about the couplets in those Ecclesiastes verses is the mixture of events for which there is a right time: birth and death, war and peace. But listed in the same few verses there are everyday activities – 'a time to plant and a time to uproot . . . a time to weep and a time to laugh . . . a time to be silent and a time to speak'. What a picture of life – relatively small things mixed up with significant events, all fitted into 24 hours of the day.
- Into such a life God chose just the right time for his Son to be born in Bethlehem: 'When the time had fully come, God sent his Son, born of a woman.'[3] At a time when the Romans had opened up the known world with well-built roads, the Greeks had brought a common language, and many Jews were scattered, taking their belief in God and their religious observances with them, Christianity was founded and spread throughout many countries.
- While it was the right time for Jesus to be born, he himself

knew also when it would be the right time for him to die, for frequently he told his followers that his time had not yet come. When he knew it had, however, we read that 'he resolutely set out for Jerusalem'[4] and he set out knowing his enemies would seize him and put him to death, but knowing also that God would raise him from death on the third day. We have seen reminders of both crucifixion and resurrection in this cathedral.
- Jesus Christ did indeed come at a certain time in history, he did die to save the world, he did rise from death and in that rising broke out of time and into Eternity. He is alive for evermore – for all time.

The nave of the cathedral has now filled with large groups of schoolchildren who are enjoying a service led by a local vicar, sometimes in loud and amusing fashion and sometimes quietly. We hear boisterous laughter intermingled with periods of quiet when the children sing, first the modern song we have already heard the organist playing, 'Be still . . .', then another, 'Here I am, Lord, is it I, Lord? I have heard you calling in the night.'[5] Two thoughts come to our minds. First, such a programme should lead the children, too, to realize there is a right time for everything – either loud laughter, or just quiet worship. There is also a time to commit themselves to the Lord; indeed, it is always the right time for this, as Scripture tells us: 'Now is the time of God's favour, now is the day of salvation.'[6] We glance up again at that amusing clock knowing how the children will enjoy watching the knights of the tournament go round and knock the one hapless figure off each time. We pray they may also realize the significance of the figure below of the risen Lord Jesus.

Around the corner from this area we find a flight of well-worn steps that are attractive in themselves and lead up to the fourteenth-century chapter house. When we have carefully ascended them we find ourselves in another very attractive place. From a single central column the vaulting is spread. The room is octagonal in shape and has huge windows, although most have lost their original glass.

Returning to the crossing we notice both new and old: a tablet commemorating the visit of Her Majesty the Queen one Maundy Thursday. The other extreme is the oldest object in the cathedral and stands in the south transept; it is the Saxon font which survived from the first cathedral. Nearby, a remarkable tomb, that of Bishop Thomas Bekynton, who is remembered with affection, has a two-tiered memorial, the figure above showing how he was in life, clothed in his bishop's robes, and a skeletal figure below reminds us that no matter how important we are in life, the time comes to each one of us to die.

Having walked through the choir and paused before the high altar to look up at the magnificent east window, we pass into the retroquire that leads to the Lady Chapel. It is peaceful here, so we stay for several moments to pray.

PRAYER

God of time and eternity, we praise you that our times are in your hands, and that you always choose the right moment to fulfil your purposes in our lives.

Lord Jesus, we thank you that when you knew the time had come for your passion, you pressed forward steadfastly, knowing your Heavenly Father was with you.

Holy Spirit, we pray you will always show us the right time to do things, the right time to speak or keep silent, the right time to weep or laugh, the right time to take action or to wait, and give us strength to act at those right times.

Everlasting Trinity, forgive us when we choose the wrong time to act or speak.

Amen

Glancing at our watches, we realize there is little of the allotted time left, so we leave the cathedral by the north porch in order to look up at the exterior clock with its two medieval warriors who smite a bell at the appropriate times. The Latin words on this clock, 'Nequid pereat' translated mean, 'Let nothing be lost' or 'Don't waste time'! We feel we have certainly not wasted time but we take a quick walk across to the bishop's palace in the few moments we have left. Standing by the moat we watch the swans as they swim towards a rope hanging down from a window above. They have learned to jerk this rope to ring a bell at the right times, that is, at meal times!

As we walk back to the waiting coach we remember one more time, known only to God – the Second Coming of our Lord. No one has any idea when this will be, despite many so-called predictions. One thing we can be certain about, however, is that it will be spot on – the right time.

8

YORK

God, our protector

There can be few better places to visit at the start of a new millennium than the city of York, brimming with historical evidence along most of its streets, around many corners and visibly commemorated in a number of locations, not least York Minster. The city was begun as a Roman fortress, built as early as AD 71, and there has been Christian worship there for over thirteen hundred years.

The minster, the chief church in the northern province of the Church of England and seat of the Archbishop of York, is the largest medieval cathedral in Northern Europe. The term 'minster' is derived from the Latin for monastery and was originally used as a missionary centre, having a team of clergy who went out into the surrounding countryside to preach the gospel of Jesus Christ. York has also been the seat of a bishop from its beginning so it has always been a cathedral.

The ideal standpoint from which to really absorb the atmosphere and feeling of history in the minster is right at the crossing, beneath the central tower, from where we can see glorious stained glass windows at four points – west, east, south and north. On a bright day, with the sun streaming through these and other windows, the stonework, the fluted pillars supporting Gothic arches, and the roof bosses on the vaulting, all seems to sparkle and the impact is overwhelming. Beauty is on every side beckoning us to explore.

Before doing so, however, we spend some moments viewing the west window, built during the fourteenth century and thoroughly repaired in recent years. It illustrates the authority and purpose of the ministry of the Church, having pictures of eight archbishops of York in the bottom row, with apostles shown above them. Scenes from the earthly life of Jesus, as preached by the apostles, are shown higher still. What is fascinating, however, is the stone tracery at the top of the window for it incorporates the shape of a heart, seeming to represent the sacred heart of Christ, so reminding people of his unique love for them and for the world. The heart shape has also given a more mundane nickname to the window: 'The Heart of Yorkshire'. Yet surely there is a basic truth here for the preaching about the love of our Lord is really central to life. Later, we discover that this heart shape can be clearly seen from the exterior as well.

We decide to begin our exploration by going back to the beginning of the history of this place, as shown in an exhibition in an area now called 'The Foundations', reached from the south transept. This space was excavated between 1967 and 1972, rather hastily because the central tower of the minster seemed likely to collapse. Engineers therefore raced against time to secure the foundations. It was while this work was being undertaken that ancient remains were uncovered beneath the minster, remains that give us a picture of two thousand years of history, the period of time celebrated at the start of the new millennium.

As we descend into this area we are, in effect, stepping into layers of archaeology, able to see some of the remains of the Roman legionary fortress, Viking gravestones and sections of the foundations of the Norman cathedral built in 1080 using stone taken from the Roman fortress. A reconstruction of a Roman road with its first-century culvert can also be seen, as well as a Roman military wall painting. There is a definite link with Christianity in these foundations, for the tribunal stage, or dais, where all major announcements were made and ceremonies conducted, lies hidden here. We know that the Roman emperor, Constantine the Great, was proclaimed Caesar in this place when it was learned that his father had been killed in battle, so it is possible the announcement was made from that platform. It was Constantine who eventually declared Christianity to be the official religion of the Roman Empire, and later we shall see his statue outside and near the south door. But it is down here that we do indeed feel we are walking through two thousand years of history.

- Two thousand years since the Son of God was seen in human flesh, having been born in Bethlehem into an ordinary family, and brought up in Nazareth, in Palestine.
- Two thousand years since his glory was seen, full of grace and truth, as he revealed the real nature of God, who is not only almighty but the loving Heavenly Father.
- Two thousand years since that glorious grace and truth was

seen in acts of healing and kindness, brought to a climax by death on a cross that secured salvation for all who believe in him.
- Two thousand years since the man Jesus was raised from death by Almighty God, endorsing his claim that he was the resurrection and the life, and that he was ascending to his Father's side to reign with him for ever.
- Two thousand years of his followers calling people to believe in him, to respond to his love, and to follow him in their daily living, so bringing them to life eternal.
- Two thousand years indicated by the change of dating, from BC (before Christ) to AD (Anno Domini – in the year of our Lord).

Although we think it may well have been Roman soldiers who first introduced Christianity to this country, we cannot be quite sure. That it was established here by the third or fourth centuries we are certain, as evidenced by the early Celtic saints and martyrs such as Alban and Edmund, whose stories are told in an earlier book about cathedrals.[1] Much has happened since those far-off days, of course, and when we return to the south transept we do not immediately linger in it but walk on along the south choir aisle to find the entrance to the crypt.

The first thing to hold our attention in this second underground area is the Doomstone, a twelfth-century carved slab showing souls being tormented in hell, which was probably part of a larger scene showing the Last Judgement. By contrast, there is a baptismal font in the eastern crypt that commemorates the baptism of King Edwin, the Northumbrian king for whom the first minster, a small wooden church, was built in the seventh century. Particularly appealing are three altars with paintings above them depicting Edwin, St Hilda of Whitby and Bishop Paulinus who baptized the king; the altar cloths show the crown of thorns, the ladder and nails, the dice and vinegar and whip, all associated with Christ's passion. A Romanesque stone carving called the York Virgin is also seen here and is one of the minster's most important treasures. Here, too, we see the shrine and beautiful mosaic of St William of York, a twelfth-century bishop who, legend tells us, prayed for people crowded on a bridge to greet him, thus saving them from injury and drowning when the bridge collapsed.

As we leave the crypt to return to the south transept we reflect on those two thousand years again, a long period that saw many difficulties, and a fair number of tragedies. During the eighth century the church needed rebuilding after a fire; there was destruction of the Saxon minster by the Normans soon after the conquest; the central tower had to be rebuilt in the fifteenth century following partial collapse. There were two fires in the nineteenth century and, much nearer our own time, lightning struck in 1984, with flames sweeping through the south transept, destroying the roof and the medieval wooden vault beneath, and severely damaging the rose window. The stonework of this window dates from 1240 but the glass was added later, at the end of the Wars of the Roses and commemorated the union of the Houses of York and Lancaster when Henry VII married Elizabeth of York. During that latest catastrophe the glass cracked into 40,000 pieces! However, it had been cleaned and restored not long before so the lead held and no glass was lost, although much painstaking work had to be done to restore it. Now, as we stand looking up at it we are thrilled to see the pattern still there, with the great marigold centre surrounded by petals and the outer ring showing alternate white and red roses, the emblems of York and Lancaster. At this time the roof of the south transept also had to be completely rebuilt, and new bosses created, the most special of which are six that were designed by young people in response to a competition organized by the BBC children's programme *Blue Peter*.

Over the two thousand years on which we have been reflecting, the cathedral has known such disasters and some people might attribute them to the judgement of God. There is, however, something different that comes from Celtic thought. It is a realization that there are indeed evil influences in the world, even spiritual battles, which must be overcome, and the only way of doing so is to call upon and trust in the protection of God himself. The Celtic word for this truth is CAIM, meaning encircling: we are surrounded by God and encircled with his love. We also recall a verse from the Old Testament prophet Isaiah: 'Like birds hovering overhead, the Lord Almighty will shield.'[2] Yet there is another thought; not only can we call on God's protection, but at a deeper level we can pray he will bring something good out of tragedies, he will triumph over them. As we look at this glorious window, one of the loveliest rose windows we have seen in this country, we can appreciate his protection and his triumph. Even as the window was shattered, then restored, so our lives can be renewed after the most horrific experiences, by God's strength.

We turn at last from reflecting on the message here and look towards the north transept, to another famous window. This is known as the Five Sisters Window and contains green and grey 'grisaille' glass in geometric patterns, representing the story of five unmarried sisters who worked tapestries similar in design. The window has over 100,000 pieces of glass in it, and it is difficult to decipher any design in it, but it is now a memorial to the women who lost their lives in the two World Wars. This transept has two other points of interest, both clocks. One is an astronomical clock given to commemorate the 18,000 allied airmen who were killed in World War II when flying out of bases in Yorkshire and the north east. The other is a striking clock with two 400-year-old figures of men-at-arms that strike the hours and quarters which we stand watching with other visitors. The clock having struck, we turn our attention to the chapter house just off this transept where the carvings are exquisite.

Back at the crossing we notice that the screen separating the nave from the choir also has a real sense of history, in that the stone statues are of 15 kings of England, dating from William I through to Henry VI.

It is when we reach the Lady Chapel that we are right up close to the other great window we have glimpsed from the crossing, and this east window extends our thinking about the past two thousand years, for it shows all of time, from its beginning when God created the world, as told in the book of Genesis at the beginning of the Bible, and on to the vision of St John in the book of Revelation at the end of the Bible, which looks ahead to the final days and the Last Judgement. The window is so detailed it is difficult to pick out events, but there is a useful chart nearby that helps identify some of them. Although two thousand years have been observed at this point in our history, we remember that God is not limited by time. Some words from a modern worship song come to mind: 'For no one else in history is like You, And history itself belongs to You. Alpha and Omega, You have loved me, And I will share eternity with You.' But that song reminds us that for the past two thousand years 'It's all about You, Jesus . . . You alone are God.' (Paul Oakley)[3]

We are looking for a quiet place in which to pray and, having passed several small chapels, come to one in which we feel we can do so, rather apart from the groups of visitors touring with a guide. It is St Stephen's Chapel, to the north of the Lady Chapel, where the reredos behind the altar is a carving of the crucifixion, and we also see the same scene in the window above, so reminding us of what the millennium is really all about. To one side of the altar is a modern carving of a woman holding a baby, but as we approach it we realize at once it is not the usual Madonna and Child, for the woman is elderly, her faced lined, although that face has a look of love and compassion. It is a sculpture of Mother Teresa of Calcutta, holding one of the babies she has rescued.

PRAYER

God of history, we bow before you, humbled by the thought of your care and the way you guard us from evil when we trust you. We believe that, because you are all powerful, you will keep us from the evil one and bring us to yourself when our time here on earth is over.

We praise you, Almighty God, that you can bring good out of seeming tragedies, and help us overcome worldly problems, because you are by our side at all times and we can know peace in your presence.

Lord Jesus, as we look at the cross with you hanging on it, we remember how the Father God brought an overcoming of evil through that supreme act of sacrifice, and raised you from death on the third day.

Holy Spirit, continue to strengthen us as we live out our time, helping us to be true to our Lord, following in his way even as people like Mother Teresa and so many others have done, by caring for the desperate people needing comfort.

Amen

Walking back through the minster, we pause near the west end of the central aisle, beside the second pillar on the north side, and as suggested by a notice here we quietly say the Lord's Prayer, a prayer that has been said daily for two thousand years. Since Jesus taught his disciples how to pray, for two thousand years we have addressed God as 'Our Father'; we have prayed that his name be hallowed, that his kingdom should come and his will be done. For two thousand years we have prayed to him for daily bread, for forgiveness as we forgive others, and that we will not be led into temptation but that he will deliver us from evil. For two thousand years we have acknowledged that his is the kingdom, the power and the glory for ever. As we leave this wonderful building, we say a hearty Amen (may it be so) to that prayer.

PART II

God the Son

9
WAKEFIELD
What was the point of Jesus's coming?

An imaginative redevelopment scheme in recent years has set the cathedral in Wakefield so much in the heart of the shopping precinct that it has become virtually part of the everyday life of the city. Office and shop workers, restaurant patrons and shoppers probably walk past or enter this splendid building every day. Nevertheless it is still possible to be aware of it once away from the city centre, for the 247-foot spire is the highest in Yorkshire.

There is a friendly atmosphere about this cathedral, one in which we immediately feel at home as we enter. We are arrested by a haze of colour, for the kneelers, rather than being out of sight, hang from the tops of the pew backs and their soft shades add to the beauty of the nave. One of the daily services is nearing its end and, although we cannot see the participants in a chapel at the far end of the cathedral, we can clearly hear the priest's words. Rather than walking about we therefore sit and listen: 'Christ has died, Christ has risen, Christ will come again.' They are words used in the Holy Communion service and bring a special meaning to the great gilded crucifix of the rood screen. Just as Mary and the apostle John standing either side of the cross did, we too gaze at it and take in the thought of evil being overcome, represented by the serpent at the foot of the cross. We feel almost like the seraphs at either end of the scene who, with two of their six wings, cover their faces, as told in the prophecy of Isaiah;[1] it is an awesome sight.

As we sit waiting for the service to end, we look up at the wooden ceiling liberally sprinkled with bosses, then at the alternating pillars of round and octagonal shapes and realize there must have been many changes to the structure of this house of God since the first Norman church was built about 1100. That early church had a low roof but some two hundred years later it was enlarged and the height increased, evidence of which can be seen by the difference in stone colour at the top of the pillars. A few fluted pillars replaced others when the tower collapsed at the beginning of the fourteenth century, destroying much of the church.

When the service is finished we are able to begin our tour and we do so remembering those words spoken by the priest that 'Christ will come again'. It is during the Advent season that Christians are particularly urged to consider the Second Coming of Christ. However, at that time of the year people are usually more interested in preparing to celebrate his first coming and to set up the familiar manger scene in which we say it happened.

Having walked down the south aisle we come to some vivid reminders of that first Christmas in the Lady Chapel, which is unusually situated here rather than at the east end behind the altar. A modern, and unusual, sculpture in this chapel has the Madonna holding the baby Jesus, but in a rather different pose than the way we usually see her, for she is seated cross-legged – surely a very natural position for a young mother sitting on a bare stable floor. It was carved by Ian Judd in 1986 and is very lovely. The stained glass window in this chapel tells the story of the nativity in greater detail. It has four lights; in the first we see Mary with Joseph arriving in Bethlehem, obviously looking for somewhere to stay; the second is the usual nativity scene with Mary and Joseph looking at the baby; the three wise men are shown in the third picture; and the fourth depicts the flight into Egypt after those magi had left Bethlehem. What is so appealing here is the way in which Joseph is portrayed as a thoroughly caring and strong man, one in whom Mary must have had the greatest confidence. We do not always give enough thought to the vital role this man played in that nativity event, and indeed in the early years of Jesus's earthly life.

- It was to Joseph, as well as to Mary, that the truth was told about the unique nature of the baby she was to bear.
- It was to Joseph that the message was given, by an angel of the Lord, about the name for the child: 'Jesus, because he will save his people from their sins' and 'Immanuel – which means, "God with us".'[2]
- It was Joseph who took Mary with him, even though she was expecting a baby that he knew was not his, when he had to travel to Bethlehem; he would be the one to find them some kind of shelter when they were told 'there was no room for them in the inn'.[3]

- It was Joseph who obeyed the guidance from God, given in a dream, to take Mary and the baby and flee to Egypt because of the brutal intentions of Herod the king. Then, when it was safe to do so, to return to Israel and settle the family in Nazareth.[4]
- It would be Joseph who trained the young lad in his carpenter's shop, and who provided for his wife, Mary, and the rest of the family. It was also Joseph who took that same lad to Jerusalem when he was 12 years old and helped Mary search for him when the boy became lost.[5]
- Surely, also, it would be from Joseph that Jesus learned the genuine characteristics of a good earthly father, things he would never forget even when he became aware that his true father was a heavenly one – God Almighty.

Leaving the Lady Chapel we walk on to the Walsham How Chapel where we find an effigy to this first Bishop of Wakefield, enthroned as such when Wakefield was given the status of a city in 1888 and the church became a cathedral. Children are particularly remembered here in a children's window and, in fact, this great nineteenth-century hymnwriter was often known as the children's bishop. Among his many compositions is the well-known children's hymn: 'It is a thing most wonderful, Almost too wonderful to be, That God's own son should come from heaven And die to save a child like me.'

What suitable words to remember in thinking about the birth of Jesus! Why did he come? Why did God the Heavenly Father send him to earth? Was there any point in it? Jesus himself once summed up the purpose for his coming in some memorable words: 'For the Son of Man came to seek and to save what was lost.'[6] And he fulfilled that purpose simply because he loved humanity. That love sent him to live among human beings, share in their everyday experiences, be with them – the meaning of Immanuel. The name Jesus, by which he was and still is known, is deeply meaningful – that even though he would himself live a sinless life, he would share the human experience of dying, so taking on himself the sin of the world, the sin of every individual, and bring reconciliation with God the Heavenly Father to everyone who believed in him and accepted the forgiveness made possible by that death. Those words written by the bishop would have helped children to understand this wonderful gospel message. We glance back at that crucifix on the rood screen and answer our own question with different words, this time from one of our modern songs: 'From heaven You came, helpless babe, entered our world, your glory veiled; not to be served but to serve, and give your life that we might live. This is our God, the Servant King.' (Graham Kendrick)[7]

Another of William Walsham How's well-known hymns is particularly appropriate to remember here: 'For all the saints who from their labours rest', for this cathedral is dedicated to All Saints, and the windows, most of which are by Charles Kempe, the nineteenth-century artist, portray illustrations of the great figures who have been true witnesses of the holy God we serve. The Bible's Old Testament can be traced in the north aisle, starting with Creation at the west end, and going through the patriarchs and prophets, then leading into New Testament scenes; as well, some of the Celtic saints who worked so tirelessly in northern Britain are seen. In the south aisle, along which we have already walked, are shown New Testament themes and figures, including all the apostles and some of the early Christians.

Before we leave the south side of the cathedral we examine a representation of an ancient Saxon open-air preaching cross that once stood by the town wall. Only the shaft remains and it was discovered being used as a doorstep in a Wakefield shop, and rescued. The shaft we now see is a plaster cast of the original and is covered with the familiar interweaving Celtic knot patterns. It is a certain indication that the Saxons worshipped here before William the Conqueror invaded. Indeed, Edward the Confessor was Lord of the Manor of Wakefield.

As we reach the east end we find ourselves in a twentieth-century extension, although the stone lierne vaulted area harmonizes well with the rest of the building. Here is a quiet place, known as St Mark's Chapel, and as it is reserved for private prayer we will kneel or sit here. The hanging, to the right of the altar, shows the traditional symbols of St Mark the Evangelist and was created by Sylvia Dawson in 1986. The Gospel of St Mark does not, in fact, give an account of the birth of Jesus, and we wonder why. Yet the message of the Incarnation is very real in that Gospel, where Jesus is so vividly portrayed as seeking out the needy, the marginalized of society, the misunderstood, the sick and suffering, and his compassion led him to bring new life to them as he spoke to their particular need. For the message of the Incarnation is about a God who has come into our world, it is the message the Celtic missionaries would have emphasized: Jesus truly became one with the people and still we can pray to him with our petitions, knowing he will understand. The challenge is that he desires we shall pray for other people's needs also, and even as he went about helping people, so he expects us to follow him in the same way.

PRAYER

Lord Jesus, we bow before your altar here in this quiet place, filled with gratitude for the way in which you lived a human life. Even more, for the way that you died to save us from all our wrongdoings.

God, our Heavenly Father, how we thank you for sending your Son to share our experiences, letting him live in an ordinary family with his mother and earthly father, Joseph.

Lord, fill us with your spirit that we may live as you lived, moved with such compassion for suffering and needy people that you may be seen in all we do. Help us, like you, to go about doing good, but doing it in your way, for only then will we begin to understand the true meaning of the Incarnation.

Amen

We walk past the windows depicting the saints who not only learned this message of the Incarnation but embraced it themselves, and we go out into the city centre, out among people going about their everyday lives, yet going about them so close to the Christian centre of this city. Jesus did not live out in the desert away from people, but among them, even as this cathedral is central to everyday life here in Wakefield.

10

PORTSMOUTH

Jesus, Prince of Peace

The thought usually uppermost in our minds when visiting cathedrals is that we are about to step into a different atmosphere, away from the scenes through which we have passed on our way, almost into another world, as it were. At Portsmouth this is not so, for the thoroughly maritime situation of the town and harbour seems to permeate this rather unusual place of worship.

The clear, extremely light nave, wide and lofty, which is a recent extension, with its attractive pillars and pale walls, is so effective that at first we simply stand still, staring around us. There are no pews or arranged chairs, just open space emphasizing the thought of mighty oceans and horizons, clear skies in which are set the stars by which seagoing vessels steer, and the overall feeling of vastness experienced when on a long sea voyage. This large open space also makes us feel we are still outside the church, although there are several views through to the older part of the building. The cathedral is, in fact, in three main styles: medieval, classical and modern.

Its history begins in the twelfth century when a certain Jean de Gisors, a wealthy Norman merchant, granted land to the monks of Southwick Priory on which to build a chapel to commemorate St Thomas Becket, who had been murdered at Canterbury just ten years previously. This medieval building served the sea-faring community in this area but it was greatly damaged during the Civil War and only the transepts and chancel now remain. It is on record that the building was used as a lookout post and lighthouse in times of both peace and war so that, when the Parliamentary forces attacked the town in 1642, the Royalist garrison was able to observe the enemy's movements from the tower. In return, the Parliamentary gunners inflicted cannon fire damage to the tower.

Neglect followed, with the medieval tower and nave falling into ruin. When the monarchy was restored, however, prosperity and expansion followed for the borough and dockyard, with strong support from Charles II. Within a few years, the tower and nave had been rebuilt and several additions made. We had noticed how attractive the tower was with its wooden cupola, and seafarers must have been grateful in 1703 when a lantern was added, as well as a ring of bells.

When the new Diocese of Portsmouth was created at the beginning of the twentieth century, what had been the parish church of St Thomas became a cathedral. By that time plans were being drawn up for an extension to the church, the chosen style being a round-arched Rhenish Romanesque to echo the style of the choir. The onset of World War II meant, of course, that the plans had to be put on hold and it was to be over fifty years before it was possible to finish the work.

Going up a flight of stairs to a gallery in order to have an overall view, we can see that the nave is encircled by both aisles and an outer ambulatory, which we realize is why the church seems so wide. From here, too, we have a perfect view of a modern statue, 'Christus', designed by Peter Eugene Ball and carved from a piece of oak driftwood partly covered with gold leaf, positioned high above the rounded arch leading to the older part of the cathedral.

Having got our bearings, so to speak, when we descend we walk across to the low vaulted north ambulatory, where we find a ship's bell at the entrance to the east end. Yet it is something still ahead that has drawn us to this area, for we can just discern a number of lighted candles on an unusual and impressive structure. Based on a design from Stockholm Cathedral and made in 1985 by students of Highbury College of Technology, here hangs the Peace Globe, the ribs of which are static, but at its heart rotates a cross, symbol of despair and of hope. Spaced along the horizontal strands of the globe are small candle holders, ready to receive a candle from visitors as a focus for prayer. We stand looking into the globe, then light our candles as we meditate.

Our thoughts, having been dominated by the sea, we remember how, for the Jewish people of Jesus's day, seas were places to be feared, believing that such depths portrayed the power that fought against the deity. They recognized, however, that the Creator God was controller of oceans and in their psalms the sea was urged to 'resound'[1] along with everyone in the world. However, they also remembered the prophet's words: 'the wicked are like the tossing sea, which cannot rest, whose waves cast up mire and mud. "There is no peace," says my God, "for the wicked."'[2] What would those Jews have thought of this globe dedicated to peace, so close to the sea?

Jesus would, of course, have been aware of their fears as he walked beside the Sea of Galilee so frequently during his earthly ministry, and it was peace he brought to people in so many different ways. As he gave the customary Hebrew greeting, 'Shalom', people would feel he was speaking something far more profound and meaningful than a mere word. He was not simply wishing them a time without conflict, but an inner sense of well-being, wholeness, harmony and order.

- As he walked beside the Sea of Galilee and saw two pairs of fishermen brothers, Simon Peter and Andrew, James and John, and called them to follow him, they experienced the peace of having a true purpose in their lives.[3]
- As he climbed into the boat belonging to Simon Peter, using it as a makeshift pulpit, and preached to the crowds gathered on the shore, his hearers knew that when they took full notice of what he was saying and followed his teaching in their daily living, they would know peace.[4]
- As a guest in the home of Simon Peter, probably a fisherman's cottage beside the sea, he brought healing to an elderly woman, giving her the peace that relief from a fever can bring.[5]
- After another intense time of preaching to, as well as feeding, a crowd of five thousand, when the disciples were rowing back across a tempestuous sea, Jesus came to their assistance by walking over the waves. Simon Peter, when he himself attempted to walk to Jesus on those same waves, learned that peace of trusting in Jesus can only come by keeping the eyes fixed on him.[6]
- Probably the most well-known story of Jesus bringing peace on the sea is that of another time when the disciples were struggling against the stormy winds and waves and Jesus was asleep in the stern of the boat. In response to their waking him, those beautiful words were spoken, so meaningful still to our troubled and anxious minds, 'Peace, be still.'[7]
- After the resurrection, again Simon Peter found peace beside the sea, when he and his friends were met by Jesus, who had cooked a breakfast of fish for them on the shore, then had a

quiet conversation with his disciple. From that talk, Simon Peter found the wonderful peace not only of full forgiveness for his denial of Jesus at his time of need, but of reinstatement as leader of the disciples.[8]

Walking back along the north side of the cathedral, we glance into the Lady Chapel, then admire a medieval wall painting which, although somewhat faded, is interesting. It shows Christ in Majesty on the Day of Judgement, assisted by the heavenly host. On a wall near the crossing we find a ceramic plaque of the Virgin and Child by Andrea della Robbia, the medieval Florentine sculptor. This prompts our memory of the prophecy which calls Jesus, among other titles, 'Prince of Peace'.[9]

From here it is but a few steps to something else unusual. Central, beneath the tower and in front of the entrance to the seventeenth-century choir, is a modern baptistry, made to a ninth-century Greek design. It is too small for the total immersion of an adult but larger than the usual font, although its purpose is for the christening of infants. Around this rectangular font is an inscription attributed to Cyril of Jerusalem: 'When you went down into the water, it was like night and you could see nothing: but when you came up again it was like finding yourself in the day. That one moment was your death and your birth: that saving water was both your grave and your mother.' Applied to the baptism of believers, those words are very significant as symbolically they die to sin as they go under the water, and rise to new life in Christ as they come up out of it, knowing also that peace of sins forgiven.

A bookstall stands near another dominant bronze statue, this time of St John the Baptist, cast in 1951 as a memorial to a Winchester college boy killed on the Matterhorn mountain. Just here also is a superb painting by W. I. Wyllie, a celebrated marine artist who lived locally. It is entitled 'The Miraculous Draught of Fishes' and refers to that resurrection scene which we have already mentioned. Near the painting we also see the original 'Golden Barque' weather vane, dating from 1710, and very striking. A replica of this barque, made in 1953, is now on the cupola of the tower, so it is good to be able to see at close hand what it really looks like.

It is time now to look for a unique area in the cathedral. This is the Navy Aisle where we find several items reminding us of our country's close association with the sea. This aisle was one of the first sections of the twentieth-century's extension plan to be finished and was partly paid for by donations received from officers and men of the Royal Navy. Farther back in history, it was in this cathedral that naval commanders received communion before taking their first appointment, as required by law until the early nineteenth century. In the floor we find the memorial to a crew member of Henry VIII's flag ship, *Mary Rose* (now on view in the harbour) which foundered in the Solent in July 1545, and was raised almost 450 years later in 1984. A model of this ship is hanging high up in this aisle. Here also is a memorial to the crew of the Portsmouth fishing vessel, *Wilhelmina J.*, lost at sea in 1991, and this is remembered again by a small commemorative window behind the bookstall.

The most meaningful part of this aisle is, however, the Holy Martyrs Chapel. The altar is dedicated to St John the Baptist and several other martyrs, with a statue of St Sebastian above the altar. This modern sculpture has arrow heads sticking out around the body, indicating the saint's torture in the third century at the command of the Roman Emperor Diocletian. He was eventually killed with clubs. Beneath the statue is a three-panel triptych bearing the imprint of a cross, which can be opened to reveal shafts of resurrection light.

A pair of windows in this chapel are extremely clear and expressive. They are known for their D-Day connections and depict the two most famous seaborne actions of World War Il – the rescue of British troops at the evacuation of Dunkirk in 1940, and the landing of allied forces in Normandy in 1944. Servicemen are clearly seen being helped into one of the small fishing craft that went to their rescue, in one of the windows, while in the other allied soldiers are shown scrambling ashore. The window is, in fact, a memorial to the man who commanded the seaborne forces in both actions, Admiral Sir Bertram Ramsay. Our thoughts of peace return to us strongly, this time not only that we personally might know the deep peace that Jesus brings, but that our powerful Prince of Peace might be known throughout the whole world, changing people's lives, chasing away evil and terrorism, and bringing peaceful stability to countries far and near.

From that feeling of being rather outside the main church, we leave behind that atmosphere of sea and sky, and come into what is now the main worship area of the cathedral. The main altar and the pulpit stand on a podium of Purbeck stone and the tester above the pulpit is surmounted by an impressive statue of the goddess of Fame. From her trumpet hangs a banner, on which is a quotation from the prophet Isaiah: 'Cry aloud, spare not, lift up thy voice like a trumpet, and shew my people their transgression, and the house of Jacob their sins.'[10] We might be tempted to feel this adds nothing to our thoughts of peace, but when we read that Old Testament chapter we discover the Lord speaking to the people who do turn to his way, 'Then shalt thou call, and the Lord shall answer; thou shalt cry, and he shall say, Here I am,'[11] and that truly will bring peace of heart.

Leaving this classical area, we move on into the original chancel, now called the chapel of St Thomas. This, the remaining part of the twelfth-century church, is of exceptional architectural interest, it being quite unusual for a church to have an east end with side aisles designed in this way. There is also quite a different atmosphere here. It is quietly evocative of those early days when the monks wished to commemorate the murdered Archbishop, Thomas Becket, by building a chapel. This being the most atmospheric part of the cathedral, we will stand here and pray.

PRAYER

Mighty God, who created all things at the beginning of time, gathering the waters together so that there were seas and dry land, we thank you for your continued control over the elements and that we are able to enjoy the pleasures of seaside, when we have respect for the deep waters and use them with care. We thank you, too, for refreshment of body and mind, and the peaceful experience of holidays.

Lord Jesus Christ, who came to this earth bringing peace to the hearts of those who turned sincerely to you, we now come to you asking for peace as you give us a purpose for our lives, show us the right way of living, touch us with healing when we need it, calm our anxieties, bring us forgiveness and help us to trust you at all times. We thank you that we can know deep peace, simply by being in your presence.

Holy Spirit, who hovered over the waters at Creation, bringing order out of chaos, we thank you that as we know your continual work in our lives, we may experience that peace and joy which comes from our experiences of you.

Three-in-one God, ever working over the powers of evil and darkness, we pray you will continue to work in our lives in such a way that

we may encourage a feeling of peace for other people as we meet them. So may a great chain of peace be joined around the entire world. This, we know, is a huge prayer but our faith in you, Lord God, helps us to cry to you, knowing you will hear and answer.
Amen

There is a new west door, made of bronze and installed at the end of 1997, above which is a rose window of plain glass but with a delightful tracery pattern. The note beside the door tells us the motif is of the Tree of Life, an ancient symbol of the endlessly renewed life force at the heart of creation. It also mentions the open expanse of the nave with its many entrances, perspectives and crossings reflecting our many-layered search for God. We feel we have indeed been close to the Lord in our search today, and have found the peace he gives.

The maritime atmosphere remains with us as we walk past the harbour where boats of all kinds, from small yachts to ferry boats and old warships, are anchored. In our hearts we add a prayer, 'For those in peril on the sea'.

11
PETERBOROUGH
Jesus the healer

The desire for health and healing has always been a priority in people's minds, as it still is. In the Middle Ages this gave rise to the cult of relics, with those who were able being prepared to go on long pilgrimages to visit shrines of holy people, even to touch the holy bones and other body parts if this were possible, in the firm belief that their ills would be cured. As well as healing powers, the protection and absolution which the saint had exercised when alive were considered to be retained by the relics and so they became objects of veneration. Saints' relics were also thought to help make a place holy and that sanctity could be 'caught', as it were, simply by touching these remains. If only it were that easy! Peterborough was a centre of these pilgrimages.

The eleventh-century Abbot Aelfsy was particularly keen on relics, and has been described as 'a laborious bee', storing them up in his abbey at Peterborough. Included in his collection, it is said, were Aaron's rod, pieces of Jesus's swaddling clothes, a shoulder blade from one of Bethlehem's holy innocents, and a piece of bread from the feeding of the five thousand! The most valuable relic, however, was considered to be the whole arm of an early Celtic saint.

The seventh-century Northumbrian King Oswald was always generous to the poor. One Easter, as he was eating his meal, he thought of the poor at his gates and wanted to help them. But there was not enough food for them all so he ordered that his silver dishes should be broken up and that each poor person be given a little of the silver to buy food. Aidan, of Lindisfarne, was with him at the time and he immediately took hold of Oswald's right arm, saying, 'May this arm which is so generous never perish.' Oswald was killed in battle at Oswestry in 642, but his right arm was completely preserved. It was kept at his castle in Bamburgh, Northumbria, for at least four hundred years. Then a monk of Peterborough, named Winegot, somehow managed to get possession of the arm and transferred it to the abbey, where it became the principal relic until the Reformation, when it was either destroyed or buried. We discovered this story of Oswald's arm, and other information, in an extremely pleasing exhibition in the north transept.

Nearby is a small chapel which at present houses the treasury, with a collection of church silver, although it is not this that attracts our attention but a relatively small stained glass window high above the exhibits. It shows several of the healing miracles of Jesus: giving sight to the blind, helping a lame man to walk, and raising the dead. It was, of course, his inspiration and indeed his command that his followers should heal, as well as preach, and as they tried to follow his example they learned that true healing only came through him – they were merely instruments through which his healing power could reach people. The saints whose relics were stored in so many of our cathedrals also learned this during their lifetimes, for we know they did exercise a healing ministry and, in fact, were only named 'saints' if such miracles, both while they were alive and after their death, could be proved.

It was certainly the recognition of Jesus as a healer that drew so many people to him and his healing was never to a set pattern, for he always met a person in their individual need, as he still does. He knew that he had come to fulfil the Old Testament prophecy, 'The Spirit of the Sovereign Lord is on me, because the Lord has anointed me to preach good news to the poor. He has sent me to bind up the broken-hearted, to proclaim freedom for the captives and release for the prisoners.'[1] In reply to a question brought to him from John the Baptist as to whether or not he was the one they had expected, he told the messengers, 'Go back and report to John what you have seen and heard: the blind receive sight, the lame walk, those who have leprosy are cured, the deaf hear, the dead are raised, and the good news is preached to the poor.'[2] As we stand here looking up at these significant windows, we ponder on the special way Jesus dealt with people who needed his healing touch.

- Even when it might be understood that he was preoccupied with thoughts of what lay ahead for him in Jerusalem, as he travelled to that city, a cry from Bartimaeus was not only heard but immediately responded to, by calling for the blind man to be brought to him. His gentle question was so courteous, as we might say today, 'How can I help you?'[3]

- His consideration for people's feelings was wonderful. When a deaf man with a speech impediment was brought to him, he quietly led him away from the crowd and carefully demonstrated to the man how he was about to bring him healing.[4]
- With his special insight, he could go right to the heart of the matter and discern just why a person was suffering in a particular way. With a paralysed man, carried to Jesus by four friends and let down through a roof to his feet, Jesus knew the man was in the grip of deep remorse and guilt. His assurance that his sins were forgiven became the means of the man's healing.[5]
- When a shy woman crept up behind him to touch the hem of his garment in order to find healing, he knew power had gone out from him to the woman, but he did not ignore her. For he knew, too, that in order for her healing to be complete, she needed to make it known.[6]
- Jesus knew how healing a simple touch can be, especially for a person suffering from an illness like leprosy. One man with this disease approached Jesus with some trepidation, knowing how people kept their distance from such sufferers, and simply asked if he was willing to help him. The joy of his healing was not only that Jesus was willing, but that he demonstrated the fact by leaning over and touching him.[7]
- It was not only physical healing that Jesus gave – and still gives. He was just as concerned for people with mental problems. In a desert place, met by a raving man, he stood firm, showing courage, and gently spoke to the sufferer, asking his name and, although there was really no need to exorcise the man's demons in the way requested, nevertheless he did so, giving the man confidence that he had been restored to a right and sane mind.[8]
- To those who mourned and were broken-hearted because of bereavement, he proved not only a source of comfort but reassurance that he was indeed the 'resurrection and the life'. We cannot understand fully or explain the way in which he brought certain people back to life, but in the story of the raising of Lazarus we get a glimpse of the way in which he showed sympathy to bereaved people.[9]

In our services for Christian healing these days, we would do well to try more to emulate Jesus's way with sick and suffering people, showing that same courtesy, understanding, and sympathy that not only endeared people to him but gave them confidence to approach him, whatever their problem.

Having had our eyes fixed on that window for a while, we now lower them to look at the silver vessels in the treasury. They remind us of another gospel story, that of the rich ruler who came to Jesus and asked what he must do to inherit eternal life,[10] a question to which Jesus replied that he should sell his possessions and give the money to the poor. We do not know the outcome of that advice but we can appreciate the reason for it; obviously this man's riches were more important to him than anything else. The message here surely is that any treasure is of little use if we do not have health, for that is of far greater value. Of even more worth is our trust in Jesus himself. We wonder, did all those pilgrims of long ago find healing, not by touching the relics of saintly people, but by turning to the Lord for whose glory these great cathedrals were built?

Turning our attention now to the nave, we look up at the large modern hanging crucifix, by Frank Roger and designed by George Pace in 1975. It is in aluminium gilt with a Latin inscription that, translated, states: 'The Cross stands while the earth revolves'. This is the place where we find true healing, we know, as we look at the cross, remembering how Jesus died to save us from all the wrong we had done, or that had been done to us, so bringing us true 'salvation', the word that also means 'healing'. As the Old Testament prophet said, 'Surely he took up our infirmities and carried our sorrows . . . and by his wounds we are healed.'[11]

Standing beneath that rood and looking down the length of the nave, with its clear glass windows, we try to discern the pattern on the unique painted ceiling, although we cannot see it to advantage until we insert a coin into a provided slot, when it becomes well lit. It really needs a very bright day to see this thirteenth-century masterpiece at its best. This is such a majestic interior and, with no screen separating the nave and choir, presents a feeling of wholeness, closely akin to that sense of healing we have been meditating upon.

For the first nine hundred years of this building it was an abbey, thought to have been founded by Peada, the first Christian king of Mercia, with Saxulf as first abbot. The site was probably chosen as a good centre from which to evangelize the region. This evangelistic work is commemorated in a carved panel on the Victorian choir pulpit, where Saxulf is shown preaching the gospel to the people of

Mercia. The monastic church was destroyed by the Danes in 870 but one hundred years later King Edgar built a second, which was the minster of a Benedictine abbey. A fire destroyed that one at the beginning of the twelfth century. Another building was begun within a few years, although it took well over another hundred years before it was ready for consecration. This is the fine Norman building we now see, although there were, of course, repairs following the vandalism of the Civil War, and a few additions over the centuries. When Henry VIII suppressed the larger monasteries, including that at Peterborough, he chose to keep this church and raise it to the status of a cathedral for the new diocese of Peterborough.

Moving into the choir, we find the stalls have Victorian carvings of figures from the cathedral's history, including the story of St Oswald. As we pass on into the sanctuary we look up to see another wonderful ceiling, yet there is something even more glorious to study a little further ahead. This is the apse, where the Norman building was started, and the ceiling shows Christ and the apostles. It was designed by Sir George Gilbert Scott, based on descriptions of the medieval original which had been destroyed by the musket fire of Cromwell's soldiers. There are also a couple of seventeenth-century Flemish tapestries that are particularly attractive. They show two incidents in the life of Peter, one in which he is seen being rescued from prison, with his chains falling of,[12] and the other as he heals the lame man who called out to him at the beautiful gate to the temple.[13]

Right at the far east end we walk around what is known as the new building, which was the last addition to the church, built at the end of the fifteenth century. The fan-vaulting is superb, and here also we find stained glass windows with clear scenes from both Old and New Testament stories. In this area we discover the only remains of the first abbey visible above ground level, a large stone dated about AD 780 and known as the Hedda, or Monks', Stone. The carvings show Christ, the Virgin Mary and some of the apostles. There are, in fact, several very interesting sculptures around the cathedral, some old and some modern. The one that most appeals to us is a twentieth-century French carving of the Good Shepherd, standing beside the votive candles.

Either side of the sanctuary and apse are aisles where two queens whose lives ended in tragedy are remembered. In the north presbytery aisle is the most famous of all the memorials in this cathedral, that of Catherine of Aragon, first wife of Henry VIII. Her tomb is beneath a plain slab flush with the floor, but we find a comprehensive history of her life in an exhibition beside it. We are intrigued to read more details about her, knowing already she was first married to Henry's older brother, Prince Arthur, while still in her teens but widowed within months of the marriage. When she later married Henry they were, apparently, in love and very happy for twenty years, but when she failed to produce a male heir, and when Henry fell in love with Anne Boleyn, they were divorced. Although we might say that the rest is history, we learn that Catherine devoted the rest of her life to the Christian faith, even though she was kept in harsh confinement. She died in 1536 and was buried here because Henry did not want the expense of a London funeral. Our hope is that this tragic lady knew the comfort and healing of the Lord she served as he fulfilled that Old Testament prophecy of binding up the broken-hearted.

The same hope is felt as we cross over to the south presbytery aisle and stand at the site of the original burial place of another tragic lady, Mary, Queen of Scots. Executed in 1587, she was buried here for twenty-five years until her son, James I removed her body and had it buried in Westminster Abbey, opposite that of Elizabeth I. On the west wall of the nave is a colourful portrait of the Elizabethan grave-digger, Robert Scarlett, who buried both queens.

There are three small chapels in the south transept and we choose to use that dedicated to St Oswald in which to be quiet and pray. A rare twelfth-century watch tower here was originally used by a monk keeping guard over the famous relic of St Oswald's arm.

PRAYER

Mighty God, who created us all in your image, willing that we should be well and strong, we thank you for the knowledge that when things go wrong and we become ill, or suffer some kind of deformity, you are with us giving strength to cope with our problems. We pray that the peace this thought brings may help in our healing.

Lord Jesus Christ, as we study the ways in which you helped people during your earthly ministry, giving them the kind of healing they needed in such a sensitive and compassionate manner, will you inspire us to follow those ways in all our dealings with people in need. Above all, remind us to keep our ears attuned to you as we do so, and give us guidance at such times.

Holy Spirit, who gives the ability to help suffering people in Jesus's name, help us to use what you give only to the Lord's glory and not our own. Also, we give you thanks for the care of medical staff, adding to people's healing.

God, three-in-one, we thank you for the measure of health we enjoy, and ask you will keep us sensible in our habits so that we may stay strong to do your will.

Amen

The last memorial we notice as we leave the cathedral is to Edith Cavell, the nurse who, as the memorial says, 'devoted her life to healing the sick and for helping Belgian, French and British soldiers to escape' during World War I, but who was shot by the Germans. She is buried at Norwich Cathedral, but remembered here because she was a pupil at Laurel Court, which overlooks the cloister.

Our purpose in visiting cathedrals nowadays may not be primarily as pilgrims seeking healing by being near or touching relics of holy people. Yet these great Christian houses can often fill us with the peace that brings healing to our spirits, simply by being in a place where, for centuries, prayer has been offered to God.

12

BRISTOL

Jesus, friend of women

When certain friends learn we are about to visit Bristol cathedral, they seem surprised. 'Why? There's nothing spectacular there,' they claim. 'If you're going to Bristol you should see . . .' and they list several other churches, all of which we realize would be worth a visit. However, having assured them we have a purpose in going to the cathedral, we set off and on arriving find their comments immediately knocked on the head for if ever there was a word to describe this cathedral it is 'spectacular', both inside and outside.

The magnificent building standing on a wide expanse of green gives us an instant thrill, and when we enter we are again amazed for spectacular it truly is. Just inside the north entrance we visit the cathedral shop and chat with the friendly and helpful lady volunteers there, asking why this beautiful cathedral is not more well known or visited. Their comment bears out what we have already been told that, in Bristol, there are so many other beautiful churches. As we later consider the background of the cathedral, however, we wonder if it may also be because, although a church may have stood on this site for over a thousand years, the actual cathedral was not really completed until the middle of the nineteenth century, whereas some of the other places of worship in the city have a longer history.

It is an unusual structure, being the only cathedral in England built in the style of a 'hall church' with nave, choir and aisles all rising to the same height, so it does appear like a great pillared hall. There are three consequences of this: the structure is, apparently, tremendously strong with all the weight in very heavy vaulting and distributed back into the building; there is a great sense of space and unity; and the acoustics are excellent – something we shall later discover to be a superb advantage.

Looking eastward through the wide nave and its aisles, with the large windows, attractive piers, a continuous ridge-rib vault going east to west leading into a pattern of lozenge shapes in the vault of the choir, we can understand a comment by Sir Nikolaus Pevsner, the well-known twentieth-century writer on architectural history. Of Bristol, he said that he considered it superior to anything else he had seen that was built in England, indeed in Europe, at the same time.

It was in 1140 that Robert Fitzhardinge founded the Abbey of St Augustine and the present building was begun at the end of the following century. The abbey was closed by Henry VIII and the nave, which was still incomplete, was demolished, but just three years later the remaining buildings became the new cathedral dedicated to the Holy and Undivided Trinity. Yet it took more than three hundred years for a plan to be drawn up to complete the nave, as well as the west towers, and it was not until the turn of the twentieth century that the high altar and choir screen were erected. Since the end of World War II, more windows have been installed and we particularly admire one showing men and women from different sections of the armed forces.

Having been told that there are over five hundred monuments in this cathedral, we are not surprised by this number as everywhere we look we see plaques and memorials on the walls. What particularly impresses us is the large number of dedications to women. Either the women were particularly godly in Bristol, or women had come into their own in this city long before the present age of equal rights!

In the north transept we make the acquaintance of Mary Carpenter, 1807–77, who apparently had a 'Compassionate eye for children of the streets, taking to heart also the grievous lot of the Oriental women . . . the last decade of her life she went four times to India.' Crossing to the south transept we find several more dedications to women. One, Ada Vachell, was the founder of the Bristol Guild of the Handicapped: 'A woman made strong by God to give: Love to the lonely, Valour to the weak, Comfort to the sorrowful.' Another, Mary Clifford, who lived from 1842 to 1919, is described as one 'in whom love to God found a sure and beautiful expression in the service of man'.

As we stand contemplating how women seem to have been appreciated in Bristol, we recall how it was in this cathedral, in

1994, that the first ordinations of women to the priesthood took place. Our thoughts naturally turn to Scripture, and we cannot escape the fact that the gospels show so clearly how Jesus raised the status of women back to the place our Creator God had intended from the beginning. At the time of Jesus no respectable rabbi would even speak to a woman in the street, let alone consider her equal to a man, but we remember how Jesus treated women.

- Mary of Bethany was encouraged to sit at his feet and listen to his teaching, while her sister Martha was urged to be less bothered about household chores and do the same.[1]
- When a Samaritan woman approached a well on which he was resting, Jesus actually asked her to draw him some water to drink, then engaged her in a deeply theological conversation.[2] He had similar conversations, again with Mary and Martha, when their brother died.[3]
- Crushed by a crowd of followers, when he felt power go out of him he insisted on knowing who had touched him, and when a woman confessed he willingly confirmed her healing and sent her away in peace.[4]
- In a town called Nain, he halted a funeral procession, told a mourning mother not to cry, then touched the coffin and raised her son to life.[5]
- In a synagogue one Sabbath, he called a crippled woman to him, put his hands on her and healed her.[6]
- Sinful women were no exception. He welcomed being anointed by one as she wept and poured perfume on his feet, then sent her away assuring her that her sins were forgiven.[7] He refused to condemn a woman caught in the act of adultery, while the shamed men who had brought her to him slunk guiltily away.[8]
- He accepted several women following him with his twelve closest disciples, as they helped to support him in his ministry.[9]

The work of women in ministry was recognized by the early Celtic Christians, we remember, with people like St Hilda being encouraged by St Aidan to become an abbess; her monastery, with both men and women under her rule, became well known at Whitby in Yorkshire. She is said to have had great energy and wisdom.

Unusually, this cathedral has two lady chapels. One is in the place we would expect to find it, behind the high altar at the east end and known as the Eastern Lady Chapel. The windows here are especially interesting, the east window, although restored, still contains medieval glass around the edge and above the niches the windows have fourteenth-century glass.

Having seen one lady chapel, we now go round to the north transept to find what is called the Elder Lady Chapel, simply because it is older than the other and was in existence at least 50 years before the Eastern was built. An inscription outside it tells us this is 'a place of sheer exuberance and fun'. It is certainly that, for many of the amusing carvings are of monkeys and other animals playing instruments, so we find several that make us chuckle, especially a monkey playing the bagpipes!

Crossing back towards the south, we pause in the choir to look at the beautifully carved misericords and look towards the high altar with its superb carved reredos. Then in the south choir aisle we stand quite still for several moments looking at a modern window. This is by Keith New and has the theme of Pentecost, its vivid colours of red, green, blue in an abstract design conveying the coming of the Holy Spirit. The guidebook makes the special point of mentioning that when 'men and women are ordained in this Cathedral, the prayer is that they should receive the Holy Spirit, the Spirit of God's empowering for service'.

We want now to take a closer look at something we have glimpsed earlier. This is the oldest feature in the cathedral, dating from Anglo-Saxon times, and before the foundation of the abbey. Set into the east wall of the transept, it is a stone found under the chapter house floor early in the nineteenth century. The carving is said to represent the story of 'The Harrowing of Hell'. There is a detailed description beside it: 'Christ, a triumphant figure with a halo trampling on the devil and a serpent. From their grasp the Saviour is drawing a figure, probably Eve. She clutches a Cross, which is held by the strong hand of the Saviour. Christ holds her hands so they may not slip, and she is being safely lifted by the Cross from darkness to light. (Eve, mother of the whole race.)'

As we stand here marvelling at the message this ancient stone conveys, we remember the credal statement that he 'descended into Hell' and the Christian traditional belief that between his burial and resurrection Jesus 'preached to the departed, treading the Devil underfoot and drawing the souls of the faithful out of Hell by the power of his cross'. This is clearly seen in the stone, and it is considered to be one of the most important pieces of Saxon sculpture in England, although there is uncertainty about its origin.

Here is, indeed, a tremendous picture of Christ, the Saviour, releasing, redeeming, saving both men and women – anyone who looks to him and clings to his cross, thereby accepting what was done there for their salvation and that of the world. The special point of the picture on the stone is that not only does sin cling to that cross, but Christ holds Eve's hands so that once she has reached out to the cross he holds her fast. Not just that, though, because he lifts her, as the inscription says, 'from darkness to light' by the power of the cross. Nothing could convey the message of Christ's crucifixion more fully than this sculpture. Christ was, and still is, the Saviour of the world.

We walk across to look at the pulpit with its strong stone portrayals of Jesus's life: nativity, baptism, crucifixion, resurrection and ascension. He alone was able to become our Saviour for he, though equal with God, went through a human life, suffered, then rose from death and is now ascended and seated at the right hand of God, his Heavenly Father.

We remember that earthly life more as we turn into the Berkeley Chapel. The beauty here so impresses us that we simply sit gazing around us. The chapel was founded in 1337 after the death of one Lady Berkeley and there are carved shields here of the Berkeley family, who were associated with this cathedral from early times. What really holds our attention, however, are the windows showing four events in the early part of the earthly life of Jesus: as a baby, as a toddler with John the Baptist, as a boy sawing wood in Joseph's carpenter's shop, and as a slightly older boy in the temple with the teachers of the Law. These pictures remind us so strongly of the importance of women in those early years: Mary, his mother who would care for him as an infant; her kinswoman Elizabeth, the mother of John the Baptist, whom he would surely have known well; again Mary, with Joseph, who sought the 12-year-old lad when he went missing in Jerusalem. Then we remember also that it was Mary who stood by his cross and for whom he showed great concern, urging the apostle John to care for her.

Thinking of those connections Jesus had with the women of his day, and remembering also that it was Mary Magdalene and her female companions to whom he first appeared at the resurrection, we will pray in the quietness of this chapel.

PRAYER

Loving Heavenly Father, who created both men and women in your image as the Bible tells us,[10] *we thank you that still you can use both to bring your message of salvation to the men and women, boys and girls, of our day.*

Lord Jesus, in gratitude for the way you welcomed the ministry of women, we pray that they may ever respond to your call to them for dedication to your service.

Holy Spirit, who came upon the women and the men that Pentecost Day and who, with the apostles, continued your work of healing and teaching, help today's women to be obedient to your call and follow your guiding at all times. Comfort them when opposition wounds them, and make your truth known to all.
Amen

As we leave this beautiful little chapel we find that girls are filling the choir stalls. Just a few years ago it was considered a good idea to encourage girls to form a choir here, so complementing that of the men and boys. This choir has become a recognized part of the cathedral's worship. As they begin to sing now, at their rehearsal, the beautiful harmonious singing really adds to the atmosphere and, yes, the acoustics are indeed proving excellent. They are singing a lovely arrangement of the old children's hymn, 'All things bright and beautiful' but they do not stay with simple pieces, going on to Mendelssohn's trio from 'Elijah', 'Lift thine eyes', especially good for female voices.

We may not use the word spectacular again, but there is something deeply moving and beautiful about the obvious dedication of these girls, and we rejoice that they and the women have been so well accepted in the worship of this cathedral.

13

BRADFORD

Beyond the cross, life after death

Music is an integral part of most cathedrals and when visiting them during the Lent period of the 40 days leading to Holy Week, we are often rewarded by hearing choirs rehearsing. Bradford is no exemption, indeed, it has a large and flourishing choir of boys, girls and adults, who sang for Her Majesty the Queen when she visited on Maundy Thursday in 1997.

The cathedral is almost tucked away in the heart of the busy city centre, but it is well worthwhile discovering this small but beautiful house of God, where there is evidence that it has been a place of worship for some 1300 years. The present building is the third on this site and was completed at the beginning of the sixteenth century. It narrowly escaped demolition in the following century when Bradford was besieged during the Civil War but the defenders hung woolsacks on the church tower to protect it from Royalist cannon fire!

There are no sounds of gunfire today, however, just the melodic tones of the choir in rehearsal. As the interior of this cathedral is mainly stonework, the sounds are not only amplified but exquisitely resounding. Bosses adorn a wooden ceiling, and surrounding it are colourful, carved angels. The pillars are fluted, all slightly different from each other.

Church and cathedral choirs have a variety of sacred cantatas from which to choose for the Easter season, none more moving than that by J. Stainer, 'The Crucifixion'. The voice of a soloist makes us pause and listen intently as he sings the words of Jesus: 'Could ye not watch with Me one brief hour?'[1] This is the question he asked of the disciples when they slept during his agony in the Garden of Gethsemane. It brings the events of the Passion of our Lord sharply back into focus as we quietly, and as unobtrusively as possible, make our way around this cathedral.

In the south transept one of the windows is particularly

poignant. It shows not only the cross on which Jesus hangs, but the crosses either side of him bearing the two thieves crucified with him. As soloists and choir sing through the cantata we recall the scene:

- The two thieves, so completely different in their attitude, one full of contempt, the other of remorse. 'If thou be the Christ save thyself and us,' cries the first, to which his companion replies, 'Dost not thou fear God, seeing thou art in the same condemnation? . . . but this man hath done nothing amiss.'[2] And as a result, Jesus tells the penitent man that he will join him in paradise that very day.
- The Roman centurion who exclaimed on seeing the way in which Jesus died, 'Surely this man was the Son of God!'[3]
- Other people tearfully watching events come to mind, particularly the women who, according to the gospel story, watched from a distance, women who had followed Jesus and helped support him in his ministry. Such women and others are also remembered in the great west window of this cathedral.
- Details of the cruel torture meted out to Jesus are seen in the window: nails, whips, hammer, crown of thorns and the garishly coloured robe put on him when the soldiers mocked by hailing him 'King of the Jews'.

All this adds up to what we now know as Good Friday, and is what makes it so solemn a day, one that should be observed with awe. Sitting here quietly, we let the words of the beautiful chorus in four-part harmony sink into our very beings: 'God so loved the world that He gave his only begotten Son, that whoso believeth, believeth in Him should not perish, should not perish, but have everlasting life.' Surely the penitent thief, and also the Roman centurion, as well as the women who believed in him would know that everlasting life. But what of the Roman soldiers and the Jewish leaders so cruelly mocking him? God's love, exemplified by the death on the cross of his son, could bring forgiveness when they believed.

We look at another of the three windows in this transept – that depicting the resurrection, showing the women who came to the tomb and encountered angels. The crucifixion scene was certainly not the end of the story, for had it been so there would have been no Christian Church and our faith would be meaningless. No, it was not the end for the Son of God, for he was raised from death three days later. Neither the cross nor the tomb in which they buried him could hold the Saviour of the world. That is the true reason for our rejoicing on Easter Sunday.

We look across to the high altar, which is quite plain except for two gilded candlesticks above the purple cloth, and two more large candlesticks standing in front of it. Suspended on a shark-fishing line high above the altar hangs a large gold cross, completely bare – no figure of Christ on it. This, surely, is the right way for the cross of Christ to be displayed now, for he is risen and alive in the world today.

The message of resurrection is a message of comfort for bereaved people, and there are several notable memorials in this cathedral. Most poignant is seen in the south ambulatory and commemorates one, Thomas Wood, an eighteenth-century headmaster of Bradford School. The inscription says, that because of the hope of the resurrection we are not to 'grieve for this man who is in Paradise'.

A more recent tragedy is remembered on a plaque in the north transept. It was erected in appreciation of the thousands of people who contributed the £4.5 million for the bereaved and injured following the disastrous fire at the Bradford City Football ground on 11 May 1985. The plaque, carved by John Shaw, is said to have at least one gold letter for each of the 56 people who died, and one white letter for every one of the more than 300 injured.

Looking back at the high altar we read, on the metalwork above it, three meaningful texts which must be clearly visible each time a communicant receives the elements of Holy Communion. They are all words spoken by Jesus: 'I am the Bread of Life',[4] 'I am the True Vine'[5] and 'I am the Way, the Truth and the Life.'[6] When we receive the bread we remember that his body was given for us. As we drink the wine we remember that his blood was shed to cleanse us from our sins. And we remember that he alone is the way to God, the truth about God and the life given to us by God.

These were the messages preached after the resurrection, first by the apostle Peter and later by the apostle Paul, both of whom share the dedication of this cathedral. Their carved figures are shown above the sanctuary, Peter with key and net, Paul with sword, book and chains. These sculptures were designed by Alan Collins and carved by a local craftsman, but the gilding was by a 15-year-old apprentice.

The stained glass windows in the north transept hold particular interest for us as they show some of the saints of northern Britain, including King Edwin, Columba, Aidan and Cuthbert, as well as Bede and Wilfrid. Evidence of the good work done by these saints of old can be found near the sacristy door in the north ambulatory, where there is a carved stone thought to be part of a preaching cross on this site over one thousand years ago. This was the beginning of Christian witness here and a church was later built, which was destroyed, probably at the time of the Norman Conquest, to be replaced by a Norman church which, it is surmised, was burned down by the invading Scots. The stones were, however, recycled and used in the building of the third, and present, church. This eventually became the cathedral in 1919 and after World War II the architect, Sir Edward Maufe, added extensions needed for the work of a cathedral, with further alterations being made in 1987.

Still thinking about St Aidan, we turn into the small chapel near-by dedicated to this Celtic saint who established Christianity in the north. Although small and relatively plain, we gasp in appreciation of its simple beauty. On one wall are three felt hangings created by Patricia Porter in the early 1990s. The three themes illustrate chapters of Celtic Christianity, one showing the island of Iona from which Aidan was sent, another the island of Lindisfarne where he set up his community, and the middle panel is of Bradford in ancient times, when it was a village at a 'broad ford'.

Attractive as these wall hangings are, however, it is the striking cross on the small altar that holds our attention. It is known as the Cross of St Aidan and was carved by Chris Shawcross, in the early 1990s. At the top are seen St Aidan and St Oswald, the king who invited Aidan to come to his realm and who acted as his interpreter. Below are shown figures climbing up the cross, representing our Christian heritage passed on by each generation. The right arm of the cross represents the developed world and some of its questions of equality, concern for the environment, homelessness and unem-ployment, while the left arm focuses on the world that is developing with its issues of justice, peace and creation. In the centre of the cross is the Celtic symbol of the Trinity – Father, Son and Holy Spirit – three repeating spirals that continually interlock, assuring us that God has no beginning nor end. The circle around the outside of the cross has two intertwining ropes, representing the material universe and the spiritual, inseparable strands that run through life. In the notes, Chris Shawcross hopes, 'that the cross gives you inspiration for your Christian journey through life'. In this quiet place, with that inspiration for our Christian journey, we sit and pray.

PRAYER

We worship you, Almighty God, maker of heaven and earth, and our creator, for your tremendous love for the world and ourselves.

Your name, Lord Jesus Christ, will always be special to us for we know it means that you are our Saviour, who died that cruel death on the cross in order to take on yourself the sins of the world, including those sins known to us.

We praise you, Holy Spirit, that we can know your presence all through life, because of Jesus's resurrection, and look ahead to that life after death when we believe in him.
Amen

As we leave the cathedral we look up at the 100-foot tower, surmounted by a weathervane with a cockerel on it, and also the cross with a woolpack at its base and Peter's keys. And we remember how, after the resurrection, Jesus met with Peter on the seashore and reinstated him as leader of the apostles, so assuring him of complete forgiveness for his earlier denial of his master. In our hearts we too seek that forgiveness, and continue to worship him with our own songs of praise.

14

ST PAUL'S, LONDON

Light to a darkened world

Inevitably cathedrals contain much symbolism, and St Paul's is a supreme example. In particular, the sight of its massive dome rising above the devastation of the city after the firebomb raids during World War II, despite the damage caused to the east end of the cathedral, was surely a sign of hope not only to the British but also to their allies. It gave credence to the proverbial British 'stiff upper lip', the belief that they would never be defeated however severe the Blitz. Even more significant, of course, are the many symbols that bear witness to our Christian faith, not least the cathedral itself, built as a place where people come together to worship God, and as many as 2,000 do that at the main Sunday services.

For city workers, the daily sight of that great dome is an inspiration and a challenge to Christian living, which my friend and I had known during the years we worked together near Fleet Street and Ludgate Hill. As we meet up again and enter this great edifice, we do so with a sense of excitement, soon to be mingled with surprise for memories are short and we have forgotten the full beauty of this place.

At first, however, we are struck by the relative plainness both of the ceiling and the clear glass windows. Yet when we look ahead, through the full length of the cathedral to the choir and sanctuary, we can see a complete contrast in the tremendously ornate mosaic ceiling, the huge carved oak canopy over the high altar crowned by the golden figure of the risen Christ standing in front of another stupendous mosaic, this time of Christ the king reigning in glory. This is, we feel, so right and again it seems symbolic – something the early Celtic Christians may have appreciated, with their power of imagination and their way of expressing their faith in symbols. Jesus came to live an ordinary human life, then, having died to save humanity and been raised from death, was received back into glory by God the Father and now reigns there with him, ascended and glorified. There is no screen separating nave and chancel to obstruct this view and, although there are a number of monuments and statues they do not obtrude but all seem, as it were, to stand back and allow the eye to travel forward, seeing only Christ in glory.

We begin our tour by walking down the south aisle where we are impressed by wall sculptures of biblical scenes. It is, however, a statue beside some of these scenes that holds our attention. This is to Thomas Fanshaw Middleton, the first Anglican Bishop of India, shown blessing two Indian children who are kneeling before him, and the reason for our interest in this memorial is that it was erected by the joint contribution of members of the SPCK (Society for Promoting Christian Knowledge) and the SPG (Society for the Propagation of the Gospel).

Soon we are standing beneath that amazing dome, known throughout the world. We are told that, together with its superstructure, it weighs 65,000 tonnes and the height to the top of the cross is 111 metres. Eight piers support the main Portland stone structure and eight arches spread the load of the dome on to the piers. We look up into its vast expanse, but neither of us likes heights so we have decided not to climb up to view it more closely. If we did reach the whispering gallery we know that our words, when whispered against the blank circular wall, would be heard on the opposite side and we agree it would be interesting to test this. Nor are we tempted to climb the 530 steps up to the golden gallery, although the panoramic view of London would be superb.

We read in the guidebook that Christopher Wren, the renowned architect of this cathedral, kept such a close eye on the work that when this dome was being built he got himself hauled up in a basket two or three times a week to watch its progress. In fact, throughout the 35 years when the building of the cathedral was going on, Wren supervised every aspect of the work. He was 76 years old by the time the dome was completed in 1708 and he watched as his son fixed the last stone in position at the top of this great cupola. Again, there is symbolism in this, of human perseverance and dedication to the Lord for whom he built.

Rather than continuing to look up into those dizzy heights, we now lower our eyes to the floor, interested and delighted to see some recent changes, in that the chairs have been rearranged so that the seating is now 'in the round' leaving what is known as the 'sunburst' open to view for the first time in many years. This is another focal point of the cathedral, being a central pavement area decorated in a compass design of coloured marble, the rays coming from a central brass grille. It carries the Latin epitaph for the architect, which is translated: 'Beneath lies buried the founder of this church and city Christopher Wren, who lived more than ninety years not for himself but for the public good. Reader, if you seek his monument, look around you.' Later we will go down into the crypt to see where this great man lies.

Just now, however, we turn towards the north transept to see something very special, which we have both remembered from our working years in the city. Having reached the Middlesex Regiment Chapel we find Holman Hunt's superb and world-famous painting, 'The Light of the World', hanging there. It was painted by the Pre-Raphaelite artist in the mid 1800s, first as a smaller picture now housed in Keble College, Oxford, and then painted again 25 years later on a much larger canvas. This later picture was sold on the understanding that the buyer would send it round the world in the interests of evangelism; in fact, it travelled thousands of miles. Eventually it was hung in St Paul's in 1904, in the south aisle. We are pleased that it has now been moved, for the picture deserves this special place, and we sit silently for some time, absorbing the message.

At first, the face of Christ as he stands, lantern in hand, knocking at the fast-closed door, seems to us to be somewhat in shadow, but as our eyes become accustomed to the shadowy area so the light seems to increase. This does not simply seem to come from the lantern but directly from Christ himself, illuminating the meaning so clearly. The title of the painting chosen by the artist reminds us of the occasion when Jesus spoke the words: 'I am the light of the world. Whoever follows me will never walk in darkness, but will have the light of life.'[1] He was attending the annual festival of Tabernacles in Jerusalem, part of the ceremony being the lighting of golden candelabra to remind the people of the pillar of light that had gone before them through the wilderness at the time of the Exodus.

- In the same way as the people so long before had life because of the light guiding them, so Jesus claimed people could only know true guidance through life by following him. His coming into the world brought life which was 'the light of all people'.[2]

- He gave both physical light to those who were blind, and spiritual light for their reading of the Scriptures, so opening their eyes to the truth.
- He gave light to their understanding of God himself, being 'the radiance of God's glory and the exact representation of his being'.[3]
- His death destroyed the darkness of evil and gave light for all who believe in him to enter into his glory when they leave this earthly life, to be with him where we are assured, 'They will not need the light of a lamp or the light of the sun, for the Lord God will give them light.'[4]

Again, those early Celtic Christians appreciated light as a symbol of God to triumph over evil.

There is, however, a different text that Holman Hunt chose for the picture. 'Here I am! I stand at the door and knock. If anyone hears my voice and opens the door, I will come in and eat with them, and they with me.'[5] The sadness on Christ's face is surely because the door to the person's heart has been closed for so long that not only are there weeds, thorns and brambles, but rotten fruit on the ground. It is obvious, too, that there is no handle on the outside of the door. In a small booklet based on the meaning of this painting, Eric Hayden has said, 'The door to our lives has to be opened from within, using the latches or locks of repentance and faith.'[6]

It may seem incongruous to quote a simple modern worship song in this place where so much glorious classical music is regularly sung, but the words are apt and, as we sit here longing for the person behind that door to open it, we find those words coming to mind: 'Lord, the light of Your love is shining, in the midst of the darkness, shining: Jesus, Light of the world, shine upon us; set us free by the truth You now bring us . . . Shine, Jesus shine.' (Graham Kendrick)[7]

An announcement is made just now that Holy Communion is about to be celebrated in the choir and we are invited to join if we so wish. We realize what a privilege this will be so we do so, along with at least 20 other people. After the service we walk right around the ambulatory, stopping first to admire the glorious wrought-iron gates that separate the aisles from the high altar; they are by Jean

Tijou, a French master ironworker employed by Wren. Commemorated in the American Memorial Chapel are those service men and women from America, and some from Canada, killed in World War II, their names being recorded in a special book here. From this point we can realistically admire the high altar that has replaced the one damaged in the bombing; its cross stands 3 metres high. Then we reach the south choir aisle and find a picture of that all-too-familiar scene of the dome of St Paul's seen above the smoke of the city on that dreadful night of the Blitz, a scene which became quite a different kind of symbol of a light to the world. For it is well known that a circle of fire surrounded St Paul's churchyard on that night but the firemen, obeying Winston Churchill's order to save St Paul's at all costs, made an all-out effort and succeeded. It seemed the whole city of London was lit up on that night of 29 December 1940, with eight of Wren's other churches destroyed. We remember our Lord's words about the Church he would build, that 'the gates of Hades will not overcome it'.[8] Buildings may collapse but never the real Church.

Opposite the picture is a reminder of that other great fire of London in 1666. It is a marble effigy of John Donne, the most famous Dean of St Paul's (1573–1631) whose words have become immortalized: 'No man is an island entire of itself.' Although scorch marks are still visible round the base, this effigy was the only figure from the old St Paul's cathedral to survive, intact, that earlier great fire, which preceded the rebuilding by Christopher Wren.

There is just one area now to investigate – it is the crypt and its entrance is nearby. Although burials are not now held here, there are some two hundred memorials to people who have made great contributions to the life of the British people. Great figures of literature, music and art as well as physicians are all commemorated here, and also those who won distinction during various wars – men like Nelson and Wellington, whose tombs are prominent. But there is one burial place we are looking for in particular, that of Christopher Wren himself and it is not too easy to find, for it is only marked by a black slab set to one side, with a simple Latin epitaph on the wall above. Could anything be more modest for such a great man? Yet, as that epitaph says, if we want to see his monument we have only to look around us.

There is so much of interest down here in the crypt, yet there is one place to which we want to return in order to be quiet for a few moments before leaving this great cathedral, and that is to once again sit in front of that remarkable painting of 'The Light of the World'. As we do so, another verse of that modern worship song comes to mind: 'As we gaze on Your kingly brightness so our faces display Your likeness, ever changing from glory to glory: mirrored here, may our lives tell Your story . . . Shine, Jesus shine', which leads us to remember how Jesus also said, 'You are the light of the world'.[9] Challenged, we want to bow our heads and pray.

PRAYER

Lord God, we acknowledge that at creation you called for light to shine in the darkness of a chaotic world, so now we pray that light may shine in our lives chasing away the gloom and disorder.

Jesus, as we remember how you called yourself the Light of the World, we ask forgiveness that too often we have turned away from you and continued to walk in darkness, rather than let you guide us and give understanding of the true way to live.

As we gaze again at this meaningful picture, we pray, Holy Spirit, you will give us the strength to yank open that fast-closed door to the living Lord Jesus, so that he may enter our hearts and bring light into our lives.

We pray, too, that his light may shine throughout the world, dispelling the darkness of wars and terrorism, and bringing people everywhere to the light of his truth.
Amen

Outside the cathedral we walk around it, threading our way between crowds of people who are always there, many of them as tourists, others leaving their places of work to begin their journeys home. We look up at the sculpture of St Paul on a Tuscan column, representing the site where open-air sermons were once preached, bringing the light of the truth to all who would stop to listen. So much here has been symbolic of that truth, and our parting prayer is that we may not just be symbolic ourselves but true witnesses to the light Christ has given to our lives.

15

BIRMINGHAM

True and just judgement

Some cathedrals have so many beautiful and interesting artefacts that a visit becomes an almost overwhelming experience, and we hardly know where to look first. Although Birmingham has but one main feature – a series of four superb stained glass windows – they are so striking and so richly coloured they dominate the entire interior. They are by Sir Edward Burne-Jones, himself a native of the city.

The cathedral is surprisingly small, having been built as a parish church in the early eighteenth century for the newly created parish of High Town. The architect was Thomas Archer, a courtier of Queen Anne, who had travelled extensively in Europe and was greatly influenced by the architecture he saw in Italy. This becomes obvious as we approach the cathedral, with its distinctive dome and cupola topping the tower. The dedication is to St Philip. By the end of the nineteenth century, such was the growth in congregational numbers that cathedral status was a possibility, so the church was enlarged and became a cathedral when a separate see was created in 1905.

Despite World War II bombing, which set the cathedral ablaze, those four magnificent windows survived, but only because of forethought. They had been removed and stored in a mineshaft on the Welsh borders. All the other windows and the roof were destroyed, so for the rest of that war prayer continued in a building covered with corrugated iron sheeting. Restoration work was by the provost of the time, J. H. Richards.

It would certainly have been a tragedy had those windows been destroyed. As we enter and see them for the first time we feel almost sorry that they are not part of a much larger structure, for not only are they rather overpowering here, but they need more space, not just to be displayed but for their message to stand out more clearly. We are uncertain in which direction to turn first, as three of the windows are ahead of us at the far east end, and the remaining one is behind us at the west end. As they encapsulate the full message of Christ, we decide to begin with his earthly birth, depicted in one of the windows behind the high altar.

So vivid are the colours that our eyes are fixed on the windows and, for the present, we look neither to left or right as we make our way towards the chancel, until we are prevented from going further by an artistic wrought-iron communion rail. And it is not until this moment that we are able to see all three of the windows at this east end clearly, the full view having been obscured by pillars.

To our left is the Nativity window, showing Mary and Joseph with the Infant Christ in the lower part, while overhead are angels shown in a curve above a sheepfold, and shepherds gazing heavenwards. To our right is the window of the Crucifixion. Christ on the cross is looking down at his mother, commending her to the care of his disciple John, both characters gazing up at him. They stand among crowds around the cross, including Roman soldiers with spears in hand, ready to pierce his side, while at the foot of the cross kneels Mary Magdalene, weeping. Her clothing is in striking orange, contrasting with Mary's blue and John's red and green.

Central is the Ascension window, the apostolic group looking up to the figure of Christ, in robes of blue and red, standing among angels. While his right hand is held out in blessing, his left is raised up, pointing to God the Father, to whom he is returning. Here is one climax to the Christian message. Jesus came from the Father, born into our world as an ordinary human baby, lived a human life, died a human death, yet because of his divinity was raised from that death by God the Father. So he returned to God, having accomplished on earth what he had been sent to do – to die for the sins of the world, that by his death that world might be saved.

The message does not end there, however, so we turn from these dramatic scenes and go back to the west end to scrutinize the fourth window – the Last Judgement scene. This is even more full of drama, seen in every figure portrayed here. Central is the Archangel Michael sounding his trumpet for the end of the world. That instrument is not held high but points forward and down, indicating that the sound is sweeping over the crowd of people below, summoning them to the judgement day. We examine the faces carefully, some turned away from the sight above, others looking up with dread; a small child clings to his mother's richly coloured robe, and a figure on the right has his back towards us, seeming like an onlooker. The whole scene is one of tension and fear, because of the chaos of the crumbling city in the background. Yet if they would fix their eyes upon Jesus seated at the very top of the window they would see, as the description of the window says, 'the humble second person of the Trinity drawing all of us into the mystery of the Father and the Spirit'. Christ sits there in majesty, raising his hand in blessing, surrounded by archangels.

The end of the world is symbolically portrayed, an interpretation of the prophecies in the last book of the Bible, Revelation, written by the apostle John. Yet although the message is of judgement for the world, remembering that we are all part of that world we realize there is individual judgement conveyed also, and the Bible fully endorses this. 'For we must all appear before the judgment seat of Christ, that everyone may receive what is due them for the things done while in the body, whether good or bad',[1] which is but one of a great number of texts that could be quoted. This, and the whole thought of death and what happens to us after it, is something we tend to shy away from, or make jokes about, but such a picture knocks on the head our facetious remarks about meeting Peter at the pearly gates! The subject remains a mystery, of course, even though Jesus gave direct teaching about it in some of his parables.

- Several of those parables warned the disciples about being unprepared for the end of time and the final judgement. Although no one, except God the Father, knows when that day will come, Jesus said,[2] we should live in anticipation of it, our lives showing the spirit of Christ at all times and not letting ourselves be led into wrong-doing.
- Judging will be as much about what we have not done as about the wrong deeds we have committed. Being blessed, have we used our blessings in the right way or buried them? Has the kind of compassion that Jesus himself showed been seen in us, ministering to people in need?[3]
- Have we been willing to turn to him in humility, accepting the forgiveness for everything in our lives that has not met God's standard, because we acknowledge that his death on the cross was to free us from condemnation?[4]

- Most importantly, as John's Gospel says, are we among those who believe in him and are therefore not condemned, or have we, as it were, condemned ourselves because we have not believed?[5]

This is how we believe judgement will be exercised, and this is how our destiny will be decided. Of all the teaching Jesus gave while here on earth, this is the most soul-searching and we turn from that symbolic picture, almost not wanting to think about it too deeply but just to get on with living our lives to the full. Stealing a furtive glimpse back at the face of Christ shown in this window, however, we can see clearly that face is shown with an expression of deep and understanding love – his judgements will indeed be true and just. He has lived this earthly life, he knows the difficulties as well as the joys it can bring, he understands how easy it must be to falter and make wrong decisions. That loving face has almost a pleading look in it. It urges us to keep our thoughts fixed on him. Looking towards the east end again, where we can just see the Crucifixion window, we remember how he himself stood in the judgement hall before the Roman governor, Pontius Pilate. He knows what it means to be judged.

We would have liked to go up into either the north or south galleries, which are still as Thomas Archer built them, but they are kept closed except for special occasions. It would have been good to look down on the nave from such a viewpoint, but also to sit up there out of sight of those challenging windows! Instead, we walk past square, fluted columns, back towards the east end, pausing to look up at the fine organ which, at present, is being tuned – something we often hear in our visits to cathedrals. Although the organ has been rebuilt a couple of times during its existence, the case is original and we are able to see some delightful carvings high up near the pipes.

We find our quiet place in a chapel at the end of the north aisle and sit in front of a modern sculpture created by Peter Ball of Newark. It is an amazing crucifix, made from a wooden railway sleeper, and copper and bronze foil. The figure of Christ exudes pathos and suffering, although his majesty is also there, as is his compassion. It is that compassion which gives us courage to come to him in prayer, for we know that not only does he hear our prayers, but he will answer because of his unique love and understanding.

PRAYER

Almighty God, we acknowledge that our lives must always be under your scrutiny and that when we leave this world we will stand before you for your judgement. We realize, too, that one day – we do not know when or how – you will judge the whole world. So we pray you will look on us in love and in pity.

Lord Jesus Christ, we thank you that because you lived on this earth you understand our weaknesses. Even more, we give you thanks that because of your death on the cross you took the consequences of our wrongs on yourself, paying the price, so that we can know forgiveness and have eternal life.

Holy Spirit, we know we cannot earn our entrance into the Kingdom in our own strength, or through any merit we have, so we appeal to you for help to live our lives here on earth in the spirit of Christ. We pray, too, that you will give us the sense to believe in Jesus, accepting what he has done for us and trusting in him completely.

Oh God, some things seem difficult for us to understand. We only know the one certainty is that we must one day face death, although we cannot be sure if this will come sooner or later. So we simply pray for your blessing, both here and for Eternity.

Amen

Crossing to the south side, we linger beside an exhibition that outlines future plans. It shows what is called the 'nostalgic past' but emphasizes how Cathedral Square is part of the city centre core, not just a place in which to work. In the 'future' section, the Cathedral Square Millennium project is outlined. An avenue of London plane trees will be planted around the perimeter, with elegant piers at the entrance. There will be new floodlighting and better lighting for the footpaths, with security and warden facilities.

The plans sound sensible, to be looked forward to. Thinking of these, and also the forethought that saved those windows from destruction during World War II, we wonder if we have been as careful about our plans for our individual and personal lives. Do those plans include sensible ways of living while we are here on earth, so that we need have absolutely no fear about what comes later, but look forward to being in the presence of the God we serve because the Holy Spirit has enabled us to commit ourselves to Jesus Christ?

PART III

God the Holy Spirit

16

SOUTHWELL

The Spirit gives life

Although television has made it possible to witness various events as they happen, probably most people would agree it is never as good as actually being present. Nevertheless, many places have been introduced to us through this medium, including some of our great cathedrals. Ever since the televising of an Easter morning service from Southwell Minster, the cathedral church of Nottinghamshire, we have wanted to visit this lesser-known but, as we could see from the programme, extremely beautiful house of God, and our visit really brought it to life.

The setting is especially pleasant, being in the smallest cathedral town in England. It is the kind of town where it is not unusual to come face to face with the Provost or other members of the clergy, as a corner of the streets in the shopping area is turned, and to be smilingly greeted. Equally friendly greetings await us in the cathedral itself.

As we enter through the north porch we feel immediately the familiarity of the building, for the sturdy-looking Norman pillars line each side of the nave, as we saw on TV. The wide round arches of the triforium above those pillars, the smaller arches of the clerestory and the wooden ceiling are all just as we remembered. Instinctively our eyes are raised to the impressive sculpture in wood, beaten copper and gold leaf, Christus Rex, showing our risen and reigning Lord with arms outstretched to welcome all who come to him. Suspended above the crossing arch, this was created by Peter Ball and given in 1987; the TV cameras focused on it frequently.

What does take us by surprise are the stained glass aisle windows, for few of these were shown during the programme. We are even more fascinated by the range of different styles, from Victorian glass to present day. Our attention, however, is immediately drawn to and held by a more recent replacement – the west window dedicated as recently as 1996. We stand looking up at the colours, which are contrastingly delicate compared to those in the aisle windows. Apparently the medieval traditions of stained and painted glass have been followed, the colours and texture being chosen to be similar to those used in the mid fifteenth century, yet the reworking of those traditions is contemporary.

It is obvious why it is called the Angel Window for there are numerous representations of these 'beings of light'. The most prominent hold spheres in which can be seen the seven Acts of Creation. There are small angels holding books and musical instruments, and higher still more angels, three with outstretched wings reflecting the Trinity. In the lower part are small scenes illustrating stories from the Bible where angels intervened, from the expulsion from the Garden of Eden through to the resurrection. At the viewing point for the window we can read a descriptive explanation on a stand (or a leaflet is available from the bookstall), which is helpful for it is difficult to see every detail from ground level. Two phrases speak to us particularly: 'Here at the foot of the window is where angels touch the earth', referring to those biblical scenes. And the opening sentence tells us this new window replaces 'a rather dull plain green and yellow window inserted in the 19th century . . . the window brings a new sense of the joy of God's light and power to the west end of the minster nave'. As well as angels, the emblems of the Holy Spirit – the dove descending and the tongues of fire – are shown, and at the very top the Trinity is again expressed. As the leaflet says, the window 'expresses the joy and power of Creation to the greater glory of God'.

We feel the window speaks of the whole atmosphere of this cathedral, for it is such an 'alive' place and this does not surprise us either, for in the TV programme new beginnings and new life were spoken of and prayed for, and the congregation was composed of all ages, with many young people present. There is nothing here that makes us want to liken the building to a musty and old museum, full only of ancient relics, for there is so much here that is new and interesting. It gives the lie to what is too often said about the Church that it is irrelevant, even dying, with no up-to-date events taking place. Just a cursory glance through the monthly magazine indicates how varied are the activities – anything from musical events and exhibitions to a children's club, a fellowship lunch, healing services, scout parades, as well as the daily services for Morning Prayer, Holy Communion, and Evensong, with all ages being catered for regularly.

The inclusion of the Holy Spirit in that glorious west window is therefore so relevant for we remember how, throughout the Bible, so often when that Spirit is spoken of it is an indication of life, strength, vigour, and particularly newness of life.

- In the very beginning, in the story of Creation in the first few verses of the Bible, we read that 'the Spirit of God was hovering over the waters'.[1] The Spirit is seen as a creative and powerful force, bringing life to the earth which until then had been 'formless and empty'.
- Frequently, in the Old Testament, we read of characters upon whom the Spirit of God comes and enables them to do great tasks, or speak powerful prophecies, many of which make people look forward and put the past behind them. 'See, I am doing a new thing!'[2] is a message often repeated.
- When the coming of Jesus into the world as a man is announced, Mary is puzzled, but reassured as she is told that 'The Holy Spirit will come upon you . . . So the holy one to be born will be called the Son of God.'[3]
- In the New Testament gospels Jesus speaks of the need to be born again by the Spirit: 'I tell you the truth, no one can enter the kingdom of God without being born of water and the Spirit . . . the Spirit gives birth to spirit.'[4]
- After his death on the cross, God raises Jesus to life again, through the power of the Holy Spirit.
- In the book of the Acts of the Apostles, the Spirit works in the followers of Jesus, enabling them to do remarkable things and leading everyone who repents of sins and trusts in Jesus as Saviour to find that same new life.
- In the life of the Church today many people are finding that same new life the Spirit gives as they commit themselves fully to our Lord, using the particular gifts they have for his service.

Where the Holy Spirit is at work, we see that new life and vigour, as we see it at almost every turn in this magnificent building. Tucked away it may be in the heart of England, not so well known as some other cathedrals, but even though its history goes back over a thousand years it has moved with the times. Founded in the Saxon period, it was rebuilt after the Norman Conquest; damaged in the Civil War but later restored. And still it is showing us new things of beauty to add to the worship of Almighty God.

So we begin our tour to take note of some of these works of art, both old and new, pausing at each colourful window as we do so, noting that many of them portray events in the life of Jesus. Near one of these that shows the Nativity and the baptism of Jesus, we stop to look at the font with a lid surmounted by a dove representing, again, the Holy Spirit coming down to earth from heaven – the sign of that new life God has sent to parents.

There are several beautiful and interesting pieces to see in the south transept. In particular, we are attracted by a large carved bass-relief showing the flight into Egypt of Mary and Joseph with the baby Jesus, by a twentieth-century Nottinghamshire artist, Robert Kiddey. Another work, a particularly strong piece, is a twentieth-century statue of the Madonna and Child standing at the entrance to the south choir aisle.

Before continuing into this aisle, we turn aside to take a close look at something else that especially attracted us in the TV programme – the chancel screen with its richly carved canopied fourteenth-century arches, through which we can pass into the choir and on towards the high altar. On the way we walk under a beautiful eighteenth-century brass candelabrum and stop to look at an early sixteenth-century brass lectern, which was rescued from a lake at Newstead Abbey, having been hidden there at the time of the dissolution of the monasteries.

Now we stand looking up at the east window, quite different from any of the others we have seen in this cathedral. The lower four lancet windows are of sixteenth-century Flemish glass and have gorgeous colours. These were originally in the Temple Church in Paris where Marie Antoinette was imprisoned before her execution and were discovered in a pawnbroker's shop in the French capital and subsequently given to the minster in 1818. Other glass in this window is Victorian. The high altar itself is relatively simple, an indication that Southwell was, and still is, a parish church and only became a cathedral in 1884.

There is something, however, for which Southwell is famous and we hasten towards the chapter house to discover what is meant by the 'Southwell Leaves'. Here we do step back several centuries into a superb medieval building and yet still there is that feeling of life. Octagonal in shape, but without the support of a central column as seen in so many chapter houses, it has a stone-ribbed vault built in one sweeping curve from wall to wall. That vault seems to us, as we gaze up at it, like an amazing great star. Yet this is not the main attraction for, covering everything – over the capitals of the slim columns that separate the seats around the walls, on gables, arches, in fact everywhere we look – is a profusion of carved leaves, and among them figures of animals or weird human faces. We ask one of the guides the significance of these leaves and are told that the medieval masons were asked to portray perfection and they decided it was only possible to find this in nature, so they chose to carve leaves. They did not have far to look for models, being so near to the ancient Sherwood Forest, so the leaves shown are mostly those that were indigenous to the area, in particular oak, maple, hawthorn, ranunculus (buttercups) and vine. And, yes, they do spell perfection, at least in the craftsmanship. But we smile as we look at some of the other figures, for they look far from perfection with grimaces shown on faces.

With the thought of the Acts of Creation shown in that new west window we remember how, on the third day of that Creation, 'God said, "Let the land produce vegetation: seed-bearing plants and trees on the land that bear fruit with seed in it, according to their various kinds." And it was so.'[5] We could spend a long time in this chapter house, examining details of these carvings and thinking of the abundance of life, with the promise of new life ever present in the seeds, but there is more to see.

As we walk back along the passageway into the main part of the minster, we pass something completely new. This is a set of miniature carvings in metal denoting the stations of the cross and, on enquiring about these, we are told they have only just been received and are to be placed in a suitable spot outdoors. They are modern in design but we are in no doubt at all what they represent, for they speak powerfully of the passion of our Lord.

We have passed by several small chapels on our tour, each one individually appealing. Near the high altar is the Airman's Chapel which has an evocative triptych above the altar inspired by a poem by Dame Edith Sitwell, while on the wall is a memorial to the

Polish prisoners of war massacred in Katyn Forest and other places in Russia in 1940. At the end of the south choir aisle, in the Chapel of Christ the Light of the World, we are quite moved to observe a father and his two young children reverently lighting candles and praying. Beside the St Oswald Chapel we see another modern, but very meaningful, statue of Jesus showing the signs of the torture meted out by the Roman soldiers.

It is, however, to the Pilgrims Chapel we turn to find the quietness we seek for praying. This is situated just off the north transept, down a few steps. It is a simple chapel but again it has that range of artistic works which span the centuries, showing how each generation has sought to bring the worship of this place into line with their times. A crown of thorns hangs over a simple central altar, a window depicts the crucifixion scene, and a woven tapestry measuring 4 feet by 12 feet on another wall is entitled, 'Saint James and the Pilgrims'. This is by Geraldine Brock and was presented to the minster in 1990, to commemorate 150 years of policing in the county by the Nottinghamshire Constabulary. St James, being the patron saint of pilgrims, is seen with the symbols of the pilgrim – staff, purse and bag. The figures on horseback are based on characters associated with Chaucer's *Canterbury Tales*. Also included in the design is the Dove of Peace, so here again we have that symbol of the Holy Spirit who is so alive in our churches today, giving such inspiration and gifting for the glory of God.

PRAYER

Lord God, we praise you for the creativity given through the Holy Spirit that not only gave initial life but constantly renews it in every aspect of creation, as well as in our own human lives.

Speak to us, through your Holy Spirit, as we read our Bibles, we pray, giving us your interpretation.

May a deeper knowledge of yourself, O Lord, give us that new life about which Jesus spoke when he said we need to be born again in order to enter your kingdom.

We pray especially that every part of your worldwide Church may know that new life and ever move forward in your way, bringing the transforming gospel of salvation to people who as yet do not know it. Amen

We plan to leave the minster now, but groups of musicians are beginning to congregate and we realize there is to be a rehearsal for an evening concert. When we learn it is to be a performance of Haydn's 'The Creation' we relax on to one of the nave seats and listen, as a soloist sings: 'And God saw the light, that it was good: and God divided the light from the darkness . . .' We absorb the glorious music, waiting until the choir comes in with the resounding chorus: 'The heavens are telling the glory of God.' Raising our eyes again to that majestic and welcoming figure of Christ above the nave arch, we remember how, according to Scripture, he it is who sustains 'all things by his powerful word'.[6]

Eventually we drive home through countryside that is colourful with spring blossom and golden with daffodils. It all does indeed look good. It has been so appropriate to time our visit during the Spring, with its annual message of new life.

17

NEWCASTLE

The Spirit Jesus taught

On a railway journey from London to the north-east of England it is interesting to note how many cathedrals can be spotted from the train windows. We have counted about half-a-dozen, the most northerly one being St Nicholas in Newcastle-upon-Tyne. Its tower, 203 feet high, is a real landmark, with a distinctive and beautiful crown. This cathedral is one of those lesser known in England and we agree it is a shame that, while some cathedrals draw the crowds, others hardly get a mention in a guidebook of the area. St Nicholas is not only well worth a visit but is beautiful, having a dignified and reverent air about it that soothes the spirit and speaks to us of Christ.

With anticipation, because the atmosphere seems to be one of quiet expectation, we walk towards the impressive rood screen with its gilt figures of Christ on the cross flanked by his mother Mary and the apostle John, with angels. Passing beneath this, we enter the choir to find skilfully carved misericords, including several dedicated to early Celtic saints, while angels are seen above the stalls and the bishop's throne. Then we move forward to stand in front of the high altar, admiring the exquisite carved stone figures of the reredos, with the figure of Christ central, seated in glory. Designed by R. J. Johnson when St Nicholas became a cathedral, it is of Uttoxeter stone.

In historical terms, this area is relatively recent for, although in medieval times the church was the most important of four parish churches in the town, it did not attain the status of a cathedral until 1882. It is generally considered that the first church on the site, probably a wooden building on a stone base, was founded soon after the Norman Conquest but it was rebuilt in stone towards the end of the twelfth century. It has twice been damaged by fire, repaired and extended. Its history includes many references to skirmishes between the Scots and the Northumbrians for this is, of course, border country.

It is also on record that Charles I was a virtual prisoner in Newcastle for about eight months, being obliged to listen to sermons aimed at his reform!

The present pulpit has beautifully carved figures of New Testament characters and was built in the nineteenth century. About a hundred years before that, the church had been emptied of most of its furnishings, tombs and monuments. That being so, there are still several to be seen, among them the effigy of an unknown knight, in the south transept, which apparently was spared because of the pleading of the parish clerk at that time. There is also a striking memorial to Admiral Lord Collingwood, the friend of Admiral Nelson, just inside the entrance. Other memorials are in stained glass windows dedicated to various local dignitaries.

It is those windows, however, that hold the greatest memorial of all, for most of them depict scenes from the life of our Lord Jesus Christ and they do it so clearly we are left in no doubt about their references. Turning first into the south choir aisle, we are gripped by one that is a real gem. The colours are greatly influenced by browns, making for a very appealing picture of Jesus teaching, probably the Sermon on the Mount. In the upper part of the window we see one of his parables, that of the sower casting the seed on the ground. It is a powerful portrayal of Jesus as teacher, sowing the Word of God, as it were. The dedication is to the Revd James Snape, headmaster of the Royal Grammar School in Newcastle, a very prestigious school. Surely there could be no more fitting memorial to a teacher than a reminder of the greatest teacher of all time, for Jesus was readily acknowledged as a rabbi (teacher) by the people during his earthly life. In the Gospels we read how they were amazed at his teaching for he 'taught as one who had authority',[1] unravelling the mysteries and the truth of the Law given centuries before by God to Moses. Most importantly, he impressed on them that the right way to observe that Law was not just by the letter, but by the spirit, so obeying the overall law of love, that they 'may be children of your Father in heaven'.[2]

Walking on a few steps towards the east end, we see another meaningful window, the east window in the Incarnation Chapel that shows Jesus on the cross, but below that scene is another of Jesus seated at table with his disciples shortly before the crucifixion. Here the colours are vivid and startling, and there is one feature that almost makes us catch our breath. It is the figure of one disciple at the far end on the right-hand side of Christ, obviously Judas for he is turning away and looking grim. He seems to be holding something in his hand, probably the bag containing the 30 pieces of silver given in anticipation of him betraying Jesus to the Jewish leaders.[3] Then we remember the verse in John's Gospel which surely must be one of the blackest in all scripture: 'As soon as Judas had taken the bread, he went out. And it was night.'[4] If only Judas had stayed to listen to the teaching Jesus was about to give to the other disciples, teaching about his death but teaching also about the one who would be given to them following that death – the Holy Spirit.[5]

- Jesus told his disciples he would ask the Heavenly Father to give them another counsellor to be with them for ever – the Holy Spirit, indicating this spirit would be a comforter, a helper, a strengthener, one who understands and has compassion.
- This Holy Spirit would teach them all things. As a teacher, he would remind them of everything Jesus had said while with them in the flesh.
- He would also testify, that is bear witness, to Jesus, so helping the disciples to be true witnesses to their master. In this way glory would be given to Jesus.
- Very significantly, the Holy Spirit would 'convict the world of guilt in regard to sin', that sin being disbelief in Jesus. This sin was further defined by Jesus by telling the disciples that if he had not come and taught people they would not be guilty, but because he had done so they had no excuse for their sin.
- The Holy Spirit, he added, would be a guide to them, particularly prophesying and showing them the way of truth.

As he spoke to them about the Holy Spirit they would recall how once, when speaking about fathers giving good gifts to their children, he had said, 'how much more will your Father in heaven give the Holy Spirit to those who ask him!'[6] Surely their prayer, as they sat at table with Jesus, would be that they might be given the Holy Spirit if he could be all these things to them.

We turn to the north side, into what is known as the Resurrection Chapel, where the main feature of the north window is the crown of thorns, symbolized as a circle, within which are other symbols of the passion, including the nails and scourge. Then we cross to the south side, into the Ascension Chapel to look at a window given in thanksgiving for the preservation of the cathedral during World War II. Thinking of the Ascension reminds us of the last recorded words of the risen Lord, when he promised the disciples they would receive 'power when the Holy Spirit comes to you'. But that power was being given for a purpose – it was that they might be his 'witnesses in Jerusalem, and in all Judea and Samaria and to the ends of the earth'.[7] No greater challenge could have been given, and those early followers of Jesus rose to it faithfully.

So much has been spoken about the Holy Spirit in our churches in recent years, and much claim made to that power promised by Jesus, which the early Christians experienced so fully. What they realized, though, was not power in a worldly sense of the word, but strength to proclaim the gospel, to bring healing to people in the way in which Jesus had done, and above all to endure hardship, fatigue, even persecution and death. Without that infilling of the Holy Spirit, and the powerful strength he brought to their lives, they could never have accomplished all they did, as we read in the biblical book of the Acts of the Apostles. This is still what today's Christians look for as they try to follow the one who told the people of his day that the Spirit of the Lord was upon him, and who called them to follow his way.

Turning away from these three meaningful chapels we pause to look up at the Thornton Brass on the wall behind the high altar. Commemorating Agnes Thornton and her husband Roger, who died in the fifteenth century, it claims to be a powerful statement of how they saw themselves and their lives in church and society. Roger Thornton was a great benefactor and the east window we have been meditating on was one of his gifts, although it has since been restored and altered. It is recorded that he had a pious spirit which enabled him to be charitable to people in need. The record of such a man makes us feel that he, too, must have been filled with the Holy Spirit.

Above the brass is a recent addition which greatly impresses us. It is a sculpture by Stephen Cox, specially commissioned in the late 1990s, and shows an alabaster disc fractured into three pieces, above a red and purple porphyry ellipse. It reminds us strongly of the broken wafer of the Eucharist and the spilled wine. The three pieces of the disc are expressive of God the Holy Trinity and speak of the love of God that is broken for the needs of the world. In an explanatory leaflet, Stephen Cox has said his sculpture serves 'as a vehicle for that which cannot be fully explained due to the elusiveness of the transcendent and the spiritual'.

Crossing to the north side we enter St George's Chapel, which dates from the fifteenth century, and here in the windows we find reminders of earlier saints, among them Aidan, who followed Jesus so closely, teaching many young men the biblical truths in the school he set up on Lindisfarne and sending them out to teach others; also Columba, Oswald and Cuthbert. We then spot a small round window, low down near the altar, and when we have left the chapel and walked past the organ case into the north transept we come to a door leading down into a crypt chapel, where we find that the other side of this window is seen above the altar here. This chapel was originally a charnel-house and was rediscovered in 1824. A tablet on the wall beside the door and short flight of steps tells us it was built in the fourteenth century to store bones disturbed by fresh burials in an over-full graveyard.

After a few moments in the quietness here, we return to the main part of the cathedral and cross to the south aisle to look for St Margaret's Chapel. Here we discover the only known fragment of medieval stained glass remaining in the cathedral, a pre-Reformation roundel of Mary breast-feeding the baby Jesus. The stillness of this chapel and the reminders that picture gives us of how Jesus came to earth as a human baby, needing the normal care and attention of any child, are most uplifting. It would be Mary, and indeed Joseph too, who would have given the child Jesus his initial spiritual teaching and awakened in him a knowledge of the Scriptures. Later, he would realize that the prophecies in those scriptures referred to himself and the suffering he must bear. The crown of thorns behind the cross on the small altar reminds us of that suffering. Such an atmosphere prompts us to pray.

PRAYER

Father God, we thank you for sending your Son, Jesus, to teach us the way you want us to live, and to die for us that we might be forgiven when we fail to live up to your standards.

Lord Jesus, help us as we study all you had to say in your earthly teaching, that we may fully understand the better way of life you were outlining. Challenge us and help us as we try to follow that way even when it is difficult, rather than giving up if we find life hard and demanding.

Holy Spirit, we pray you will so fill us that we may know your counsel, your comfort, your understanding and, above all, your powerful strength. Remind us constantly of Jesus's teaching, that we may be good witnesses to him. We even pray you will always convict us of the wrong things we do, and guide us in all ways.

Hear our prayer in the words of a modern Christian song: 'Thank you, O my Father, For giving us Your Son, And leaving Your Spirit – Till the work on earth is done.'[8]

Amen

Having crossed the busy road outside the cathedral to the Post Office, we realize we are now standing in a building erected with the stonework that was removed 200 years ago when the cathedral was relieved of much of its furnishings. It probably makes little difference to the atmosphere of this modern facility, but we pray the inspiration of the Holy Spirit we have just experienced in the cathedral may remain with us and, even as that tower is such a landmark, may we be seen always as Christians.

18

RIPON

The Spirit given at Pentecost

Many of our cathedrals are inextricably linked with a person, perhaps because of the architecture, an event, or farther back in history someone founded a Christian community on the site. Ripon is a typical example and, as I come from Sussex, I am particularly excited about visiting this cathedral because of its close ties with St Wilfrid, who was mainly responsible for bringing the gospel to my home county.

As soon as we enter and begin to walk along the north aisle, therefore, we hurry to reach the north transept to look more closely at a window we already realize has a special significance. The Pilgrim Chapel is quite open and it is here we find the Wilfrid window. It relates to incidents in the life of this seventh-century saint who was educated at Lindisfarne, but who travelled to Rome and became enamoured by everything he saw there, including the great stone buildings, the music and art, the ceremonies of the Church, and other contemporary ideas. So it was that, on his return to England, the king of Northumbria gave him a small monastery, or mission station, that had been planted in what had been the heathen village of Rhypum by the Abbot of Melrose, who had the young Cuthbert with him as guest-master. The monks were turned out of Ripon by the king and Wilfrid brought stonemasons, plasterers and glaziers from France and Italy to build one of the first stone churches in England, dedicating it to St Peter. This was a minster, ministering to the people.

It was Wilfrid who was prominent at the Whitby Synod of AD 664, when it was decided to adopt the Roman way of dating Easter. He later became Bishop of York but on more than one occasion he fell out of favour and had to leave the area. Because of these enforced absences he travelled widely, including making a visit to the south of England where he did primary missionary work among the people of Sussex, who at that time were pagan. He arrived on the south coast at a time of famine and began his work in a realistic manner by first teaching the natives how to catch fish and make fishing nets, before teaching them about Christianity. This made his work very successful. Some of the highlights of Wilfrid's life are portrayed in the window, which was designed by Harry Harvey and placed in this chapel in 1975.

As we are standing here, the chimes of noon are heard and an elderly priest climbs into the pulpit, calling visitors to prayer. We slide into a pew near the pulpit and listen to quite the loveliest prayer we have heard in this kind of setting, as the priest remembers recent events in the life of the nation, and continues with a prayer for the peace of the world, but also for peace in our hearts. He concludes by inviting people to say together the Lord's Prayer, after which he pronounces the blessing.

The pulpit has looked attractive from where we have been sitting so now we take a closer look at it. It is modern, dating from 1913, in art nouveau style, and is bronze with marble supporting pillars. The four beautifully carved figures on it are of Saxon saints and the sounding board used to be a table top!

Eager to see the only part of Wilfrid's church remaining, we cross the nave and near the nave altar we find a narrow spiral staircase, the entrance to the crypt. It is not an easy descent but well worth negotiating the stairs, for here is something truly amazing. It is believed to be the size and shape of the tomb from which Jesus rose on the first Easter Day. There are several niches around the walls, each one filled with a light, so it is not difficult to look around. The atmosphere down here is not gloomy, just comforting and peaceful.

Except for this crypt, which would originally have been beneath the high altar, Wilfrid's church was eventually destroyed by the Danes and the monastery disappeared. A second minster was built soon afterwards but this was destroyed by the Normans, although they soon built a new church and dedicated it to both St Wilfrid and St Peter, and it became a collegiate church. In the twelfth century, the minster was again rebuilt, this time in the Norman Transitional style, the entire rebuilding being funded by Archbishop Roger de Pont l'Eveque with a gift of £1,000. There have been other disasters leading to repairs throughout the centuries, such as most cathedrals have known, but the building we see today is very much the same in plan as that of the twelfth century. It was not until 1836 that the minster became a cathedral for the then newly created diocese of

Ripon, the first diocese to be created since the Reformation.

Returning to the main part of the cathedral, we stand in front of the amazing choir screen. With just one exception, the colourful figures in the niches date from only 1947, having been created to replace those destroyed in 1547 after the dissolution of the college of canons. They represent important people in the cathedral's history. The one survival of that earlier destruction was the original representation of God the Father, still to be seen in the hood of the archway. Above the saints, bishops and kings are angels playing musical instruments, also painted in a variety of colours. We do not go through the screen just now but turn into the south choir aisle where something startling has caught our attention.

It is the screen leading into the Holy Spirit Chapel. Made to a modern design by Leslie Durbin in 1971, the striking metalwork represents the coming of the Holy Spirit at Pentecost, as recorded in the New Testament book of the Acts of the Apostles. Both the tongues of flame and whirls of wind are shown. The design is repeated in a smaller form in front of the altar. Sometimes modern designs do not please if we are traditionalists at hearts, but this is attractive because it reminds us clearly of what happened on that occasion. It was when those earliest followers of Jesus were all together soon after his ascension that they suddenly heard 'the blowing of a violent wind' that seemed to fill the whole house, and saw what 'seemed to be tongues of fire' resting on each one of them. As a result, we read, they were 'filled with the Holy Spirit and began to speak in other tongues as the Spirit enabled them'.[1]

Much has been made of this speaking in tongues in some of our churches in recent years, although some of what is said differs rather from this account of what actually happened at that Pentecost time. What is so obvious here is that the observers were amazed because they each heard the apostles speaking 'in our own native language'. They could all understand clearly the good news the apostles were telling about Jesus.

This sets us thinking about why such a gift should be given at that time. Surely, it was for no other reason than that those followers of Jesus, who had been told by their master to 'go and make disciples of all nations . . . teaching them to obey everything I have commanded you',[2] were being given the most important resource to carry out this command – to be able to talk to whoever they met in a language they could understand without the need for an interpreter.

- Jesus himself was the perfect communicator, often speaking to the ordinary people in parables, so making his message clear in stories about daily happenings, but also having more academic conversations with scholarly people like the Pharisees.
- The apostle Paul, who went over much of the known world of his time, was an educated man who could readily bring the gospel to people in many places, speaking to them in a language familiar to them.
- The early Celtic leaders recognized the necessity of being able to communicate clearly. St Aidan travelled widely throughout the north of England and must have welcomed the help of none other than King Oswald, who translated the message into Anglo-Saxon for the people Aidan met.
- During the sixteenth century, William Tyndale translated the New Testament into easy-to-read English – and went to the stake for his trouble! But the people soon had the Bible available to read in the language they spoke daily, rather than only in Latin, and Britain gradually became a different and more developed country as a result. Thomas Cranmer was responsible for The Book of Common Prayer, also written in English instead of Latin.
- Towards the end of the eighteenth century Robert Raikes of Gloucester recognized the need for children to be taught Christian truths in a simple way they could understand, so he started a Sunday School.
- Many of our modern worship songs used in churches nowadays have been welcomed because the understanding of faith and belief is expressed in everyday and up-to-date language. Modern translations of the Scriptures have helped new Christians grasp age-old truths, but have also awakened those who have been familiar with them from their youth to some deeper meanings.

Those tongues of fire were so significant to the early Christians as they planned how to spread the message of Jesus far and wide. Likewise the violent wind, because it would, as it were, blow their message around the world. They really did become Christ's witnesses, locally in Jerusalem, throughout their immediate locality – in Judea and Samaria; as well as 'to the ends of the earth',[3] and they were able to do so in the power of the Holy Spirit.

Quietly we leave this meaningful small chapel by a side entrance and find ourselves close to the high altar. The reredos is magnificent. It was designed by Sir Ninian Comper as a memorial to the dead of World War I and, because of the way we have been meditating, the alabaster, painted and gilded figures are very significant. Either side of the central figures of the Virgin and Holy Child, are those representing the two strands of Christianity that were the means of evangelizing Britain during the first millennium. On the immediate right of the Virgin are Christian leaders associated with the mission from Rome, beginning with Augustine, while on the other side are the Celtic saints, associated with the mission from Iona, beginning with Columba. There are also some smaller figures which include the Venerable Bede who so ably put into words the account of these missions. These were the people who spread the good news about Jesus Christ throughout our land – Augustine and his converts in the south, Columba and his followers in the north. The one they preached about is shown above, in an unusual manner, for here is no bearded Christ with flowing locks but a clean-shaven risen Lord with short hair, his hand upheld in blessing. On the walls either side of the altar are featured the co-patron saints of the cathedral, St Peter and St Wilfrid, each of them fishermen in their own way, yet each a 'fisher of men', bringing people to Christ.

Beyond is the glorious east window with its beautiful rose window at the top, the tracery and colours superb. Following the collapse of the east end in the late thirteenth century, this window was created under the direction of Archbishop Romanus, but the glass is Victorian. It is difficult for us to decide to turn from the high altar but when we do so we have other things to admire. Magnificent carvings abound, including roof bosses, fifteenth-century choir stalls carved by a Ripon man who was paid sixpence (2½p) a day, canopies, bench ends and misericords.

In front of us is the organ and an interesting story tells that when it was rebuilt at the end of the seventeenth century the organist's seat was moved. Unfortunately, from this new position, he was unable to conduct the choir so, in order to overcome his problem, a large pedal-operated wooden hand was put in place for the choir members to watch as the organist controlled it. Although it is no longer used, the hand can still be clearly seen and sets the mind almost thinking of parables of the hand of God, such as expressed by the Psalmist: 'As the eyes of slaves look to the hand of their master . . . so our eyes look to the Lord our God till he shows us his mercy.'[4]

Turning now to the north side of the chancel we go into another small chapel, this one appropriately called the Wilfrid Chapel. The triptych over the altar is a copy of a painting by the seventeenth-century artist, Rubens, and the window is especially clear. Here we can give thanks for a man who did so much to spread Christianity in our country, as well as for countless others who have done so before and since.

PRAYER

Mighty God, who makes yourself known to people of every age, we thank you that Wilfrid responded to your call, establishing this great church to your glory.

Lord Jesus, who gave a great commission to your followers before ascending to your Heavenly Father, we thank you that their response was to spread the message of salvation, made possible by your death on the cross, and win people in their thousands to become your disciples.

Holy Spirit, our thanks to you for keeping alive that commission throughout the centuries so that followers of Jesus are still going out to tell the good news about reconciliation and forgiveness. We pray you will continue to give strength to every Christian to speak to people in ways they can understand and accept, so that the Kingdom of God may spread around the world.

Triune God, humbly we bow before you and dedicate ourselves, as the early Christians did, to letting people know whose we are and whom we serve.

Amen

Walking away from the chapel and down the north aisle, we are reminded of several New Testament stories, seen in the stained glass windows: Jesus blessing the children, Jesus with his disciples in a boat, Jesus teaching, Jesus healing the nobleman's son. Such stories can be told over and over again and never lose their freshness if spoken as the Holy Spirit inspires.

Outside the cathedral the wind is strong, even gusting, reminding us of that mighty rushing wind of Pentecost, and in our hearts we repeat our prayer that we may have ready tongues, as Wilfrid had, to tell the stories of Jesus.

19

CHELMSFORD

Spirit of repentance

When visiting cathedrals we are usually so eager to enter and see what kind of impression the interior makes on us that, too often, we give the exterior only a cursory glance, then afterwards regret this, realizing we have missed things of interest and importance. This does not happen at Chelmsford, however, for there are two features outside that attract us, one immediately we reach the cathedral and the other that is pointed out to us.

The south porch, by which we are to enter the cathedral, is faced with stone and flint inlay, giving a chequered effect. The flints were taken from the chalk sub-strata and knapped so that the glassy black inner layers could be arranged to form the patterns. It is a two-storey structure dating from the fifteenth century when access to the upper storey was probably through an aperture and ladder. Over the centuries it has been used to house a variety of items, but is now a library reached by internal stone stairs. It also specially commemorates the US forces who were based in Essex during World War II and was therefore enriched in 1953. The cathedral's link with America is further remembered because of an association with Thomas Hooker, who was the town lecturer and curate of Chelmsford during the early seventeenth century. Although his monthly sermons in the Puritan tradition were very popular with the people, they were frowned upon by church authorities, so he fled to Holland, and from there sailed to Boston, subsequently becoming known as 'The father of American democracy'.

The other fascinating feature, which we are shown by an excited young boy whose mother is a volunteer worker in the cathedral, is a carving high up on the south-east corner of the south transept, and at once we see the reason for the little lad's enthusiasm, for here is something quite unusual. It is a modern interpretation of the apostle Peter, shown seated among his fishing nets with his catch in one hand and a modern key – of the Yale lock variety – in the other, and he is wearing large wellies!

Taking a final look at the flint and stone walls and a glance up at the eighteenth-century lantern and spire, we go inside and experience an immediate feeling of uplift. The organ is being played gently, there are several other visitors sitting quietly listening, and the whole place seems bright, clean and uncluttered. On entering, we turn our heads to the right to see a small gable window high up depicting the Holy Spirit; indeed, the atmosphere seems to speak of the presence of the Holy Spirit.

This cathedral has a three-fold dedication: St Mary the Virgin, St Peter and St Cedd. The first church to be built on this site, and dedicated to St Mary the Virgin, was founded about eight hundred years ago, but rebuilt in the late fifteenth and early sixteenth centuries. It was not until 1914, however, when Chelmsford was created as a new diocese to meet the needs of the growing population east of London, that the church became a cathedral. Its dedication was extended to St Peter and St Cedd some forty years later, and we will be reminded of all three saints in our tour.

The building has suffered a great deal of damage and vandalism over the centuries, with some of its finest work destroyed during the Civil War. Restoration work took place over the following three hundred years and during the twentieth century changes and extensions have been made to make it more suitable for use as a cathedral for the diocese, although it is still relatively small. There have also been a number of pleasing modern additions by today's artists and crafts-people, and we turn to our left to look first at the especially impressive St Peter's Chapel.

The striking bronze sculpture in the centre shows clearly that the chapel is a memorial to those who suffer in this world. Entitled, 'The Bombed Child', it is of a woman holding a small lifeless child across her knees, her face sad with eyes staring straight ahead. It has been called a bronze pieta, obviously linking it with the more usual depiction of Mary holding the crucified Christ in her arms after he had been taken down from the cross. It was sculpted by Georg Ehrlich, who was himself displaced from his native Austria following the Nazi invasion of 1938. The west window here shows the patron saints of the armed forces.

It is, however, the large south window that catches and holds our attention. This has been superbly etched, by John Hutton, with a larger than life-size figure of the apostle Peter, this time in traditional style. Surrounded by fishing nets, he stands holding keys in his left hand, for Jesus told him, we remember, that he would be given 'the keys of the kingdom of heaven',[1] and his right hand is pointing heavenwards. This, surely, is very much how Peter would have appeared on that great Day of Pentecost, just after the Holy Spirit had suddenly come upon the followers of Jesus. People watching were astonished and wanted to know what was happening, so Peter stood up and preached his first sermon, telling them that prophecy had been fulfilled, that Jesus of Nazareth, although a man, had been accredited by God, but although they had seen his miracles, wonders and signs, the people had allowed him to be handed over to wicked leaders who had put him to death on the cross. But God had raised him from the dead, and Peter and the rest of the apostles were witnesses of the fact. Now they had received the promised Holy Spirit. He finished by making the bold statement that 'God has made this Jesus, whom you crucified, both Lord and Christ.'

Deeply moved, the people wanted to know what they should do about it, and Peter's succinct reply was, 'Repent and be baptized, every one of you, in the name of Jesus Christ for the forgiveness of your sins.'[2] It was a message Peter was particularly confident to deliver, for he knew about repentance.

- It had been a clear call from John the Baptist, to whom people had flocked in their crowds to be baptized as 'repentance for the forgiveness of sins'.[3]
- Peter would remember how one day, when he and his brother Andrew were mending and washing their nets, by the Lake of Galilee, Jesus had walked along the shore with his message: 'The kingdom of God is near. Repent and believe the good news!'[4] Peter soon realized that the call to repent was more than a suggestion for people to feel sorry; it was a call to a complete turn around of their lives, from self-centredness and perhaps even evil-doing, to a commitment to God and his way of living, so coming under the rule of God and accepting that rule in their hearts. Therefore, when Peter heard the further call of Jesus, to him personally and his brother Andrew, as well as to their partners James and John, he wholeheartedly followed this man who was preaching, teaching and healing people.
- We remember how Peter was an impetuous man, often putting

his foot in it, perhaps causing Jesus a certain amount of frustration. The extreme patience, however, of his master as well as Jesus's unfailing love would have always made Peter repent again.

- Peter would remember so many other people who, having listened to Jesus's teaching and believed in him, had repented and were baptized by the disciples.[5]
- More than anything else, Peter would remember his own failing when he denied, at the moment of Jesus's greatest need, that he had ever known him. What had so filled him with remorse then had been the look Jesus had given him, a look that must have been full of love and forgiveness, a look that brought full repentance from Peter.[6] Then, after the resurrection, when he had met Jesus on the shore once more, had come the assurance of forgiveness because of that repentant spirit in Peter.[7]

Peter had changed so much from the impetuous but terrified follower of Jesus to the bold preacher, in his turn calling people to repentance, and he had done so through the power given him by the Holy Spirit that had been seen to fill both him and all the other followers of Jesus. As a result, 3,000 people responded to his message. It was a message he was to continue to preach throughout the rest of his life, a message still preached by those who try to present Jesus as Lord and Saviour, a message that still calls for a response. We look back at that meaningful sculpture of the mother and child and think of the thousands of people who have contributed to the suffering in the world today, and know it will only be through repentance that we can look forward to a better world.

Moving away from this chapel we stand looking down the length of the nave, amazed at the ceiling which is so different from anything we have previously seen. This colourful roof was part of a rebuilding programme early in the nineteenth century after a disastrous collapse of the nave due to an excavation in the vaults. Painted a deep blue, the ceiling has intricate patterns and was coloured and gilded in 1961. The result is a most effective addition to what is, overall, a beautiful small cathedral.

In the front of the nave we pause for a few moments to sit and look at the pair of very modern ambos (twin pulpits), designed in a sweeping, curved shape in steel and bronze. Above each is an interesting small icon-style cross, one conveying the cross and entitled, 'Jesus of Nazareth' and the other, 'The Cross of the Seven

Doves', representing the seven gifts of the spirit, both created by Sister Petra Clare.

Eventually we move into the chancel to look more closely at the modern altar made of Westmorland slate and weighing one-and-a-half tons, then at the bishop's chair, or cathedra, which is also a contemporary sculpture in stone and stands beneath the nineteenth-century east window. Behind the chair is an amazing hanging, suitably entitled, 'Glory', its colours inspired by those in this east window. The work of Beryl Dean, who has contributed so much artistic work to this cathedral, it is a large patchwork composed of 1,500 crosses, sewn together in a kaleidoscope of colours. The theme of praise is conveyed admirably through the impact of the colours which converge towards the central yellow, symbolizing the glory of God. Everything in this area is light, even the choir stalls being in a pale wood.

Turning to the north side and into a small chapel-like section, we find another of Beryl Dean's works, an exquisite golden banner. This is the result of over 800 hours' work. On a background of Indian cloth of gold we see the figure of the Virgin Mary, depicted in Byzantine style and holding the infant Christ; the symbols of the Trinity, the Holy Spirit and the Star of Bethlehem surround her, as well as interlacing angels' wings.

From this area we have an impressive view of the clerestory windows in the chancel through fifteenth-century twin pointed arches enclosed within a wide semicircular fan arch. We are also interested in a monument to Thomas Mildmay Esquire, a wealthy son of a businessman who lived in Chelmsford during the sixteenth century. He is shown with his wife and family, and the Latin epitaph is worth noting; it calls seven girls and eight boys, '15 pledges of their prosperous love'.

We are even more interested in a nearby window depicting St Alban and St Cedd and realize that the reason St Alban is included refers back to the time during the nineteenth century when Chelmsford was linked with the diocese of St Albans. With St Cedd, it is of course quite a different story, for he was one of the monks trained by St Aidan at Lindisfarne, who was eventually sent to Essex to become Bishop of the East Saxons. He set up Christian centres throughout the diocese, building churches and establishing monasteries; one of his churches, St Peter's-on-the-Wall at Bradwell-on-Sea, still survives.

We walk along the north aisle towards the chapel dedicated to St Cedd. Outside it we find an intercessions board, and something else that is most moving. This is a bronze plaque entitled, 'Christ the Healer' and is another work by Georg Ehrlich; it clearly shows Jesus bending to put his arms around a leprosy sufferer. It is not very large but extremely meaningful, and we remember the story of how the man came to Jesus and knelt before him with the words, 'If you are willing, you can make me clean.'[8] The compassion of Jesus overflowed to him, making him more than willing, and the man was healed of his leprosy. That was a physical cleansing but we realize, too, that many who came to Jesus were cleansed inwardly of sins when their repentance was genuine. St Cedd's chapel is the place in this cathedral recognized for private prayer.

PRAYER

Lord God, even as your preachers of old urged their hearers to repentance, we would think again of the necessity to respond to such a message. We say we are sorry, but we know that is not enough, and so we pray you will give us strength to turn around and live a better life, if ours has been going in the wrong direction.

Lord Jesus, we thank you that, because of your death on the cross, we can know we are fully forgiven and reconciled to the Heavenly Father.

Holy Spirit, even as you filled the early Christians and gave them power to witness to the grace and love of Jesus, we pray you will fill us, too, so that the Christian spirit may be seen in us.
Amen

As we leave this small and rather plain chapel, we look across to the south aisle again, taking special note of the magnificent window in Pre-Raphaelite style by Henry Holliday, giving the impression of the passage of the human soul along the steep path of life and through the river of death to its final joyful reception into Paradise. The colours are particularly rich and apparently inspired Beryl Dean's designs for the kneelers, which are also her work.

Although the outside of this cathedral initially impressed us so much, the interior has been even more inspiring. In honesty we acknowledge that, even if we make a good outward impression on people, God looks into our hearts, wanting to find repentance when necessary, and above all deep belief in him.

20

LIVERPOOL

Spirit-aided Prayer

So often when looking at a cathedral we are told we are in the largest, finest, oldest church in the country, or the windows are the most beautiful, the tower or spire the tallest, the nave the widest, or there is some other claim that makes the particular cathedral we are visiting special. At times these claims make us raise a quizzical eyebrow, but that is certainly not the case in Liverpool's Anglican Cathedral Church of Christ. It really is the largest cathedral in Britain, and to date the fifth largest in the world, being 600 feet (201 metres) long, covering an area of 104,275 square feet, with a 331-foot (101-metre tower). The bells are the highest and heaviest peal in the world, the largest bell known as Great George weighing nearly 14.75 tons. The organ has nearly a thousand pipes.

Usually there is some comment to make on entering a cathedral, even if only a few words, but in Liverpool we just stand gazing, speechless. We are completely awestruck by the great piers, soaring arches, superb windows and high roof that is so far above us we can barely discern a pattern. Despite this overwhelming atmosphere, however, we feel at once that we are in a friendly place, a house of God that is open and welcoming. Not only is this emphasized by the courteous volunteer guides on duty, but by the architectural design. No screen separates the nave from the choir, and that wide nave adds to the spaciousness. There is, too, a variation on the more usual style of a cathedral in that the shape is a double-armed cross, with two transepts each side of the nave. This special shape has become a logo for the cathedral and appears on the volunteers' badges and robes, on leaflets and, in fact, everywhere.

Despite its vast size, or maybe because of it, there seems to be a quiet restfulness wherever we go that, together with the welcoming feeling, urges us to immediately – as soon as we have got our breath back – walk right through the nave and choir, until we reach the sanctuary where we stand admiring the gilded reredos behind and above the high altar. It shows the central tenets of our Christian faith with particular emphasis on the crucifixion and the resurrection. But it is nearer eye level that we find our gaze fixed. Here is a representation of the Last Supper, with Jesus standing blessing the bread and wine, while the disciples are grouped round him, looking a little preoccupied, probably because of what he has been telling them and wondering how he can be speaking of his death.

We step back from this deeply moving central theme of the gospel to look at a pair of paintings, one either side of the choir, portraying two of the most-loved parables spoken by Jesus during his earthly ministry. These are by Christopher Le Brun and were given by the Jerusalem Trust. One, showing the Good Samaritan, reminds us of mercy and compassion, while the other, portraying the Prodigal Son, represents forgiveness and homecoming. Attention to detail is exquisite, even to the inclusion of a small dog welcoming the wanderer.

Retracing our footsteps we stand in the central space under that great tower, chatting to one of the guides and from what he says we realize how well planned is this cathedral in that it is so adaptable, both for civic occasions and for great worship events, with moveable choir stalls and other useful designs. As we stand here and look across to the visitors' centre in the north-west transept, we are intrigued by the aerial sculpture of the billowing sails of the 'Spirit of Liverpool' designed by Keith Scott. The connection of cathedral to the seafaring traditions of the city is therefore emphasized.

In the north-east transept we find the war memorial chapel, much changed during the time of the construction of this cathedral, for the period covered both World Wars. The diocese of Liverpool was formed in 1890 out of the ancient diocese of Chester and the first bishop was Bishop Ryle, who used St Peter's Church as his cathedral. This was not, however, really suitable and different ideas came with the appointment of the second bishop. He was Bishop Chavasse and under his leadership the decision was taken, in 1901, to build a new cathedral. Designs were invited from a number of architects and the winning one was by Giles Gilbert Scott, grandson of the well-known nineteenth-century architect Sir George Gilbert Scott, and only 22 years old at the time. His design was in the Gothic style and the foundation stone was laid by His Majesty

King Edward VII in 1904. The Lady Chapel was finished six years later and became the centre for worship until the first part of the main cathedral – the high altar, chancel and eastern transepts – was consecrated in a special service attended by His Majesty King George V and Queen Mary in 1924.

The second phase of the cathedral was, amazingly, finished and used for the first time in 1941. In fact, although Liverpool suffered badly from enemy bombs during World War II the cathedral escaped almost unscathed. Eventually, in 1978, Queen Elizabeth II attended the service of thanksgiving and dedication of the west end of the cathedral. Altogether, the building had taken 74 years to complete. Here in the War Memorial Chapel we remember the human toll of the two World Wars experienced during that period, from the 40,000 servicemen of Liverpool who died in World War I, commemorated in a special book of remembrance, to the many seamen who served in the Battle of the Atlantic of World War II, remembered by the bell of the warship HMS *Liverpool* hanging at the transept entrance. Beneath this entrance arch is the cenotaph, constructed of Hopton wood and black fossil marble, its sides carved with shields and canopied figures. At each corner is a small kneeling figure of a soldier, sailor, airman and marine supported by tiny angels.

We turn from these solemn memories into what must be the smallest place within this enormous cathedral, and yet the most special. It is the tiny Chapel of the Holy Spirit. A Gothic-style arch leads to an altar where the reredos almost makes us gasp with a feeling of emotion because of its beauty and depth of meaning. It portrays Jesus in solitary prayer on a mountain top overlooking the Sea of Galilee. This, surely, gives us an insight into the habit of Jesus early on in his ministry when, according to the gospels, 'Very early in the morning, while it was still dark, Jesus got up, left the house and went off to a solitary place, where he prayed.'[1] We wonder how he prayed at that time. We have a record of his later prayer, on the eve of his crucifixion,[2] as well as the way he prayed in the Garden of Gethsemane.[3] There is also, of course, what we call the Lord's Prayer, which he gave to his followers and which we still pray today. But what would he have prayed as he looked down at the Sea of Galilee at the start of his ministry? In the corners of the frame of this picture we can see the flame and dove, symbols of the Holy

Spirit, and this gives us an indication. Rather, it reminds us of what the apostle Paul told us to remember when we want to pray in difficult circumstances but do not know how to begin. He told the Christians in Rome that 'the Spirit helps us in our weakness. We do not know what we ought to pray for, but the Spirit himself intercedes for us with groans that words cannot express.'[4]

Jesus was led by the Spirit, as we sense in the gospel story, and would therefore know the deep needs of the people to whom he was to minister, making him realize the enormity of the task ahead of him and the strength needed to fulfil the will of the Heavenly Father. In order to accomplish all that he had been sent into the world to do, he needed frequent and long periods of prayer, and no doubt that prayer was often accompanied by groans that words could not express as he saw the distress of so many people around him. He is our perfect example for prayer.

- When we are faced with what seems like a gigantic task, which we know we cannot tackle in our own unaided strength, we begin with prayer.
- When we are starting a new venture and feel rather nervous or apprehensive, we can know, as we pray, the Lord's continuous presence.
- When family demands crowd in upon us and we hardly know which way to turn, how to avoid disagreements, what to advise, how to allocate the chores, whose needs to attend to first, through prayer we can know guidance from the Holy Spirit.
- When illness threatens to disrupt our routine or call for dedicated care of the elderly, a disabled member of the family, or a sick child, we pray not just for healing but for a strong and calm approach that will help the situation.
- When there is a bereavement, either in the family or to a close friend, we pray for the right kind of comfort to convey.
- As we read our Bibles, we pray that the Holy Spirit will enlighten us, so that we may discover the deep things God is saying through Scripture. Then, because of what we learn, that he will show us, if that is what we are called upon to do, the messages he would have us bring to other people.

We realize that prayer is our priority in all things of life, even if we do not really know the words to use, and as the apostle Paul goes on to say: 'he who searches our hearts knows the mind of the Spirit, because the Spirit intercedes for the saints in accordance with God's will'.[5] All that is needed is that we are sincere in our praying.

Looking up at the small stained glass windows at the side of the chapel we see various saints pictured, including Chad and Cuthbert, both early Celtic Christians from Lindisfarne, and both men of prayer. We have few records of the prayers these early saints prayed, but we know there would be simple beauty and a rhythm in the words that was almost poetic, for this is the style of Celtic prayers.

Returning to the central space we stand looking in all directions at the magnificent stained glass windows. The west window expresses the 'Benedicite', a hymn of praise to God from the natural world. Then turning around we look through the choir to the east window depicting the Te Deum and with distinctive tracery indicating the Tree of Life, but also a reminder of the Tree of Calvary. Both windows, although different in style of design, also show Christ in glory. The windows at the sides of the nave portray events in the earthly life of our Lord. Indeed, in whichever direction we look – north, south, east or west – we see the glorious Christ. Little wonder this huge edifice seems so full of his presence.

We approach a volunteer guide who kindly unlocks a gate so that we can ascend a long flight of wooden stairs to the Dulverton Bridge above the nave. The space at the top of this bridge is wide, enabling us to have a wonderful bird's eye view of the various parts of the cathedral, helped by some interesting conversation with the guide. We look around at the great walls built from local sandstone, marvelling at the skill of the craftsmen, some of whom spent their entire careers on this project.

Although the first part of this cathedral to be built and used was the Lady Chapel, we have left it until last to visit. As we make our way towards it, having descended to floor level again, we pass a wall memorial to Bishop Chavasse in the south choir aisle. It shows the bishop at prayer and again we wonder what was the gist of his prayers? We feel they would have been for the cathedral that would be built and the work that would be done in it, and we are sure those prayers must have been sincere.

The approach to the Lady Chapel is via a staircase from a gallery opening out of the south choir aisle. When we reach the lower level, we find an unusual and deeply evocative piece of modern art.

Called 'Redemption', it is an expression by a Merseyside sculptor, Arthur Dooley, and embroiderer, Ann McTavish, who had a close working relationship and discussed this interpretation of Scripture for several years. It was not, however, until after the death of Arthur in 1993 that Ann had a vision which led her to use one of his sculptures and add her own work to it. She has gone on record as saying that she tried to convey the 'feeling of the power and wonder of the event' and she has certainly achieved that for we see a small sculptured figure of the risen Christ standing on a rock, and a mass of torn textiles behind him, a perfect portrayal of what happened through his death. 'The curtain of the temple was torn in two from top to bottom.'[6] This was the dramatic happening which showed us for all time that there is no barrier to our coming to Almighty God in prayer, no need of a mediator, no curtain barring our way, for Jesus has opened up the way for us to approach God in prayer direct, wherever we are and whenever we wish, and we know he will hear us and answer.

We move into the chapel and sit or kneel near the altar, beside a much older piece of art, a statue of the Virgin Mary by the fifteenth-century Italian sculptor, Giovanni della Robbia. She, too, is kneeling in prayer and we now join her.

PRAYER

Almighty God, humbly we bow before you, thankful that we can come to you with both joy and sorrow, knowing you will listen and understand even though we may feel our words are weak.

Loving Lord, we thank you that you taught your disciples to pray and approach God by calling him Father, praising him and asking that his will should be done on earth as it is in heaven, requesting our daily bread, begging forgiveness that we might forgive others and pleading not to be led into temptation but be delivered from evil.

Holy Spirit, continue to help us in our weakness because we do not always know how to pray and you can intercede for us.

Three-in-One God, listen to the cries of our heart and when you hear, forgive.
Amen

Leaving the Lady Chapel and the cathedral itself, we determine to do what several friends have advised and walk the three-quarters of a mile along Hope Street to see the other twentieth-century cathedral to be built in Liverpool, the Roman Catholic Metropolitan Cathedral of Christ the King. The architectural contrast is so marked that once again we are speechless, both before we enter and when we see the interior. We walk all around the circular sanctuary, pausing particularly in front of a large mosaic showing the Pentecost scene when the early disciples received the Holy Spirit.

We realize that much prayer has been made here, too, with the result that there is the kind of relationship between the two cathedrals that encourages united prayer and praise. It must be a fine sight to see the Hope Street procession from one cathedral to the other at Pentecost, a sight that our Lord himself surely rejoices in for part of his recorded prayer before he left the earth was that Christians might be one, even as he and the Heavenly Father are one.[7]

21
SHEFFIELD
Unity in the Spirit

Many of our cathedrals almost tell us their own history as we view them, first externally, and then as we step inside and let our eyes take in several different types of architecture and furnishings. Sometimes it seems like reading a history book, simply to look at the various features, history that stretches from the Saxon or Norman period to the present time. Sheffield is a typical example of this diversity of style, although the Norman church here was replaced during the fifteenth century, and has been extended and altered a number of times since then, only becoming a cathedral in 1914.

A recent replacement immediately attracts us as we enter. This is the lantern roof in the narthex tower, a renovation that became necessary because of deterioration over the years which allowed rain to seep through and splash on to the floor below. The new glass is now triple-glazed and in a stainless steel structure. From the roof hang sculpted strips that suggest the crown of thorns thrust on to the head of Jesus by the jesting soldiers during his trial. The glass above is shaded from dark and sombre tones to bright arresting colours representing night and day, or death and life. We stand beneath the tower gazing up into it, realising its message that our Lord's suffering was to bring us from darkness into the light of life with him.

We are, however, equally attracted by a splendid window beyond this tower. Originally this was the west window of the cathedral but it was moved to its present position when there were plans to dramatically change the structure. Those plans had to be postponed because work was due to begin on 4 September 1939, the day following the declaration of World War II, and although some work has been done since that war ended, the plans have been modified.

The major part of the window has a salutary message. It depicts the story told in the New Testament book of the Acts of the Apostles about the vision the apostle Peter had when he was staying in the town of Joppa. As a Jew he was horrified when he seemed to hear a voice telling him to kill the animals, reptiles and birds he saw in his vision and eat the flesh, for that would be considered eating something impure or unclean. The clear message came to him, however, 'Do not call anything impure that God has made clean.'[1] The story takes up a full chapter in the Bible and the account of Peter's subsequent visit to the Roman Centurion, Cornelius, is vividly told. We remember that Cornelius is described there as God-fearing, being devout, generous and a man of prayer. But, it seems, he did not realize the significance of the life and death of Jesus, so he felt led to send for Peter who explained to him how 'God anointed Jesus of Nazareth with the Holy Spirit and power, and how he went around doing good and healing . . . because God was with him.'[2]

Peter went on to explain how Jesus had been raised by God from the dead and had commanded his followers to tell people that everyone who believed in him could receive forgiveness through his name. To Peter's amazement something incredible followed this preaching, for there were clear signs that the Holy Spirit, which he and his fellow believers had received at Pentecost, had come to this Roman soldier and the life of Cornelius was completely changed. The full meaning of his vision was therefore now clear to Peter – God has no favourites, he accepts everyone who does right and turns to him, whatever their nationality. It was a tremendous lesson for the Jewish Peter to learn, as it would be for the Roman Cornelius. Is it any easier for those of us in the present time, in a Britain that has become so multi-racial?

- Are we able to accept and try to understand the customs of people from other cultures, and do they find it difficult to fit into our society and observe our festivals, even as they hope we will allow them to keep their own?
- As we strive towards Church unity, are we able to realize there may be certain beliefs and activities in other Christian denominations from which we can learn more truth?
- In our dreams of a more just society, can we rise above our class distinctions and treat everyone we meet on equal terms, whatever their status? And can we do this without a patronizing attitude, or a false humility?
- Are we able to ignore discrimination of age or gender, and encourage both old and young, male and female, to play their part in our lives as God our heavenly Father calls them to do?

We can find a clear answer to these challenging questions in one of the apostle Paul's letters to an early church, where he tells them to be humble, gentle, patient, 'bearing with one another in love'. Then he goes on to urge them to 'keep the unity of the Spirit through the bond of peace'.[3]

Yes, it is only with the help of the Holy Spirit that we can fully achieve all that unity means, and that Holy Spirit is portrayed in this glorious window, high above the scene we have been considering. Other stories taken from the book of the Acts reminding us of both Peter and Paul are also shown in the window. These are appropriate as this cathedral's dedication is to St Peter and St Paul. The six lower lights give us scenes from the life of Jesus.

We turn now and walk down the central aisle of the nave towards the choir and the high sanctuary, standing for a few moments to look at the east window that is devoted to the memory of James Montgomery, a prolific hymnwriter. He was a newspaper editor who also helped to develop Sunday School work. Although he died in 1854, some of his hymns are still included in our books, among them one about the Holy Spirit which contains the prayer: 'O Spirit of the Lord, prepare All the round earth her God to meet',[4] a thought that echoes our meditation and our prayer that people from every nation will come to know the God we worship and adore.

We look briefly into the Lady Chapel and St Katharine's Chapel, either side of the high sanctuary, then return to the nave and enter St George's Chapel, which was at one time intended as the high sanctuary had it not been for the last war. As we mount the steps and walk towards the altar, however, we can see a window beyond that attracts us, makes us retrace our steps, turn left and make our way down to the Chapel of the Holy Spirit. Again, this chapel was originally designed for something different – namely the Lady Chapel. It is a quietly beautiful place in which to be still and meditate yet again. Having passed through the doorway surmounted by the dove symbol of the Holy Spirit, we now sit in the stalls to study the spectacular window over the altar which we had glimpsed from St George's Chapel.

The work of Christopher Webb in the first half of the twentieth century, it is called the Te Deum window and illustrates that ancient hymn of praise. Some of the verses are illustrated, and others are shown written on scrolls. At the very top is seen the Holy Spirit involved with the Creation, as told at the beginning of the Bible: 'the Spirit of God was hovering over the waters',[5] which reminds us that the Spirit plays a vital role in all of our life. Central is the figure of Christ in majesty, surrounded by cherubim and seraphim who, according to this hymn of praise, 'continually do cry holy, holy, holy'. Christ is flanked by prophets and apostles. In the lower part of the window we see the Virgin and Child, groups of martyrs and representatives of the 'Holy Church throughout all the world', as the Te Deum puts it. Our prayer is that the second verse of the Te Deum may soon be realized: 'All the earth doth worship Thee: The Father everlasting'. We continue to pray.

PRAYER

Father everlasting, we pray that people of every nation may hear the gospel of Jesus Christ and accept the wonderful news that his death on the cross was for them all.

Lord Jesus, even as you did not turn away from anyone who came to you, whatever their status, help us to treat everyone as equals, leading to yourself those who seek a true meaning for their lives.

Holy Spirit, fill us with your understanding that we may know how to live our lives and give us the strength to follow our Lord ever more nearly, day by day.

We do indeed praise you O God, acknowledging that 'Heaven and earth are full of the majesty of Thy glory' and that you are 'The Father of an infinite majesty' whose 'honourable true and only Son' we worship, and 'also the Holy Ghost the Comforter', praying that indeed we will 'never be confounded'.

Amen

The way from the Chapel of the Holy Spirit back to the cathedral entrance is not straightforward, and we pass several different chapels *en route*. Having been told about some of the work still to be accomplished here, we realize that one day there could be a greater unity in the structure. Nevertheless, we do sense a feeling of unity among the people who serve and worship here, and a loving acceptance of all who enter, seeking to know more about our God. For even as there have been many changes in this house of God throughout the centuries, so there have been many changed lives through the power of the Holy Spirit. As we leave, we glance again at the window showing Cornelius and remember his changed life.

22

DURHAM

A Spirit-filled life

However many times a visit is made to a cathedral, there always seems to be something more on which to focus, to draw spiritual help from, to meditate upon or see a meaningful aspect in the architecture or history associated with it. When circumstances are different from a previous visit, this can be particularly marked, as we experience at Durham. An earlier visit had been made on a chilly, rainy Saturday in early summer, with tourists crowding into the building away from the inclement weather, together with groups of overseas students each with their own leader trying to explain the details in simple terms and turning for help from the cathedral's voluntary guides. Our next visit is quite a contrast.

The bell is being tolled for Evening Prayer as we enter on a warm, sunny weekday afternoon and participants are already seated in the choir awaiting the clergy. We decide, however, to join just a handful of visitors who have chosen to sit in the nave, from where we can easily hear the service because of the public address system. For a little under half an hour, therefore, we quietly sit listening, while at the same time taking in the atmosphere of this, one of the most well known of our English cathedrals.

The view is uncluttered through the nave and beyond the open screen into the choir as far as the high altar and the rose window at the far east end. The stone vault is supported by massive carved pillars, 6.6 metres round and an equal measurement in height. Each pair of pillars is decorated differently, in geometric pattern, something we have always found meaningful here in that everyone is welcome, whatever their differences of nationality or creed. Indeed, this thought sets our mood for, while this is truly a building of grandeur, we do not feel awestruck or overwhelmed by it, just thrilled by the ethos of Christian fellowship and encircling warmth generated by centuries of prayer and worship. The feeling of comfortable peace stays with us as the service ends and we are free to walk around.

There would be no Durham cathedral had it not been for St Cuthbert, we have often heard, yet we want to add there would have been no northern saint like Cuthbert had he not known God's Son, Jesus Christ, and been filled with the Holy Spirit. Undoubtedly it was the realization that Cuthbert was a man who lived in close communion with his Lord that inspired the monks of old to reverence his memory and to honour his request that, should they ever have to leave Lindisfarne, where he had been bishop, they would take his remains with them (see Chapter 1). Added to that was something they realized was a miracle when, on opening his coffin eleven years after his death, his body was found to be free from decay, looking the same as on the day when it was buried. When Danish raids forced the monks of Lindisfarne to flee some two hundred years later, they therefore took his body in a wooden coffin and wandered about the north of England for over a hundred years until they found a safe place on a rocky piece of land almost entirely surrounded by the River Wear.

We may smile at the story of how the monks settled on this spot, but it bears remembering. As they came near to the place we now know as Durham, the coffin they carried suddenly became so heavy they could not move it. Then one of the monks had a vision in which St Cuthbert indicated he wished to be buried at Dunholme, but they did not know the location of this place. Two local peasant women were then heard calling to each other, one saying she had lost her cow, and the other replying she had seen the cow on Dunholme. Greatly excited, the monks asked the women to show them the way to that place and this time the coffin was easy to move. Sure enough, when they reached the spot the cow was discovered and the monks knew they had found the final resting place for the saint. They therefore built a little temporary church over the coffin, made of the boughs of trees – the first Durham Cathedral! Later, when we go back outside, we will see a stone carving of this story on a corner at the north-east end.

Within a few years a new building, called 'the White Church', had been erected and became the shrine of St Cuthbert for nearly a hundred years, until it was pulled down for the foundations of the Norman cathedral we know today to be laid by Bishop William of St Calais and the Benedictine monks. As well as the body of St

Cuthbert, the coffin contained the skull of St Oswald, the king who had invited Aidan to Northumbria to evangelize his people and who was later killed in battle. The new shrine behind the high altar was completed at the beginning of the twelfth century. Throughout the Middle Ages pilgrimages were made here but at the Reformation the elaborate shrine was broken up and St Cuthbert's coffin was eventually buried below the spot where the shrine had stood. Since that time, a plain marble slab has marked the place and we will see this later.

Just now we turn back towards the north door through which we entered and from which we had an immediate reminder of St Cuthbert in a clear and beautiful stained glass window ahead of us, showing the saint surrounded by his beloved birds. It leads us on and down into what is known as the Galilee Chapel. Part of this is also called the Lady Chapel, unusually situated here at the west end because the bishop at the time it was built became sure the saint did not wish the chapel to be at the east end of the cathedral near his shrine! The whole area is, in fact, divided into three quite different chapels.

At the north side as we enter, we can clearly see a twelfth-century wall painting behind the altar, again showing St Cuthbert. Next to it is the chapel of our Lady of Pity, with a modern statue of the annunciation. The third chapel commemorates another early saint, for here is the tomb of the Venerable Bede, who died in AD 735 and whose bones were brought to Durham about three hundred years later. This scholarly monk from Jarrow who gave us so much by writing the early history of Christianity in our country, and who told us great details about those early Celtic saints, especially St Cuthbert, has a fitting verse above his tomb: 'Christ is the morning star who when the night of this world is past brings to his saints the promise of the light of life and opens everlasting day.' According to one of the cathedral's leaflets, this is a quotation from his commentary on the book of Revelation.

Moving back to the first chapel, we sit here looking at the wall painting of St Cuthbert, remembering his life and meditating on the kind of person he was.

- Like the Lord he served, he was a man of prayer, often spending whole nights praying, and seeking the kind of solitude where he could fight the battle of good over evil through deep and concentrated prayer. We remember how Jesus spent nights in prayer, in particular when important decisions had to be made,[2] and especially just before facing death.[3]

- Cuthbert was a lover of nature, as Jesus was.[4]
- Even as Jesus's response to people was so often because he was 'filled with compassion' for them,[5] Cuthbert was a man of great compassion, helping people find forgiveness for what they had done wrong, and bringing them healing of body and mind. Also, like Jesus, he travelled far and wide in his concern for people in remote areas needing help.
- He must have borne in mind his Master's teaching about being a peacemaker, for at a time when the Celtic Christians were deep in debate about recognizing the Roman way of observing certain Christian practices, he carefully led the people in his charge in a calm manner.
- Obviously Cuthbert possessed the spiritual gifts of healing and teaching, but more noticeably he showed the spiritual fruits of love, joy, peace, patience, kindness, goodness, faithfulness, gentleness and self-control,[6] living by the Holy Spirit as Jesus had done. As a consequence, people flocked to him for spiritual counsel.

All this can, of course, be summed up by the clear indication that Cuthbert simply tried to live as Jesus had and to follow his teaching. The Spirit of Christ could be seen in him to a marked degree.

Having left the Galilee Chapel by its south door, we are now standing beneath the south west tower so we continue walking along the aisle in front of us, first turning to look back at the companion window to that of St Cuthbert. This one on the south side shows St Oswald, King of Northumbria, holding a cross as his sword. Another cross in the background represents the one he put up in view of the enemy at the battle of Heavenfield, which he won, thereby claiming the northern kingdom and helping to bring Christianity to the people.

As we proceed along the south aisle, we glance through a door towards the cloister, where the Treasury is situated which houses, among other things, Cuthbert's beautiful little pectoral cross, and the wooden coffin in which the monks carried his body for all those years. The cloister reminds us that, until 1540, this was the church of the Benedictine monastery where the monks worked and worshipped.

Just beyond the door, we stop to look at a striking memorial. It is in memory of the miners of County Durham 'who have given their lives in the pits of this county and those who work in darkness and danger in those pits today'. There is a miner's lamp at the side and a book of remembrance.

When we reach the south transept there is something else fascinating to admire. This is the clock provided by Thomas Castell, who was prior here at the turn of the fifteenth century. Amazingly it survived vandalism by thousands of Scots prisoners taken by Oliver Cromwell after the battle of Dunbar and shut up in the cathedral. Half-starved and exhausted, with no coals allowed them, they broke up all the woodwork they could find, including the choir stalls, in order to make fires for warmth. It is thought they spared the clock because it has a carving of the Scottish thistle on it, but many people consider the prisoners just wanted to keep in touch with the time! After the Restoration, Bishop John Cosin did considerable restoration work in the cathedral.

There are a number of interesting stained glass windows throughout the cathedral and in the south choir aisle we look at the latest, named the Millennium Window. As well as commemorating Cuthbert, it also shows Durham industries and trade, and characteristically a bishop is seen leaning forward to shake hands with a miner.

Walking under the great central tower, which was completed in 1470 after the original had been struck by lightning, we come into the choir with its intricate carvings and pass the bishop's throne – the highest in the country. Then we stand before the high altar and admire the fourteenth-century Neville Screen, given by a family that was one of the most influential in England throughout the Middle Ages. Made of Caen stone, the screen originally held 107 richly gilded and painted statues of saints, but all these were lost at the time of the dissolution and never found. The altar itself covers an earlier marble one placed here by Dean Hunt at the beginning of the seventeenth century, and this small Jacobean altar is still used at certain times of the year.

So we reach, at the far east end, the chapel of the nine altars, which was built in the mid thirteenth century. It was designed in a series of bays and the reason for the original nine altars was to accommodate the many priests in the monastery at the time, for their daily saying of Mass. Nowadays this is mainly just a spacious area, but from here we can look up and see more detail in that glorious rose window. We have been considering St Cuthbert, and other great Christian leaders, as we have toured the cathedral, but here is the reminder – if we needed one – of the one to whose glory this great edifice was really built, for in the centre of the window is seated Christ in Majesty. It is indeed he who reigns over all, both here and in the universe. He is surrounded in the window by the apostles, and in the outer ring by the 24 elders mentioned in the book of Revelation.[7]

The floor just here is lower than the main body of the church, and we have therefore to climb a short staircase to reach the special place of pilgrimage, St Cuthbert's Shrine. Beside the plain grey slab on the site of the saint's ancient shrine stands his statue, and he holds the head of St Oswald in his hand. As we sit here thinking of the story of this saint who did so much to bring the good news of Jesus to the people of the north, a group of young people enter, each lighting one of the candles and stooping down to pray at the shrine. It is a very moving moment and our own prayer is that these young Christians will look beyond the saintly man of God and worship the Lord he served so faithfully and truly. We add our own personal prayers.

PRAYER

Mighty God, we thank you for the example of those Christians, both of old and of modern times, who challenge us to live in the way you intended we should when you put us into the world. Forgive us when we fail to try to match that high standard.

Lord Jesus, we are humbled when we remember people like Cuthbert, but we thank you for the story of his life and the inspiration he was and still is. Help us to be as he was, people of prayer, compassionate for those in need, lovers of creation, and peacemakers.

Holy Spirit, we pray you will so fill us with yourself that other people may see in us the true Christian spirit, that we may be the kind of witnesses to Jesus who will draw them to him for themselves.

Trinity God, Father, Son and Holy Spirit, we praise you that you fill this great place built to your glory. You who care for us in a

parental way, you who walk with us in our daily living, you who inspire and strengthen us, keep us always conscious of your presence, so making our lives the most worthwhile they can be.
Amen

We want to linger here, just being quiet and reflecting on the Lord's majesty and goodness, but other visitors are coming up into this place so we leave space for them, descending the steps on the north side, and walk towards the exit along the north aisle. As we go out of the main door, we turn to look at something that is well known, the sanctuary knocker, a reminder of the Middle Ages when criminals on the run could grasp hold of this knocker and claim sanctuary in the cathedral. It signifies a peaceful refuge, something we can so often be aware of even today as we visit cathedrals and churches, and which we can always know when Jesus Christ lives in our hearts.

It is good to make return visits to cathedrals, for then we can usually enjoy a different experience as we focus on other aspects of the building, or its story, to that noticed previously. Even as Jesus used parables to make a point, this thought can help us appreciate it is not always an initial looking at the Christian message that brings its truth home to us, but as we return to it and think about it more deeply.

GLOSSARY

Cathedral The word comes from the Latin *cathedra*, meaning a seat or chair. A cathedral is the principal church in a diocese (an Anglican district) in which the bishop has his seat, more generally known now as his 'throne'. A cathedral is usually built in the shape of a cross, the stem lying east to west, the main part being the nave with an aisle on each side. The two arms are known as north and south transepts. At the east end, the head of the cross, are the choir and high altar. The main entrance to a cathedral is nearly always at the west end. Cathedrals and monastic churches were, in earlier days, built for the use of Christian communities where canons, monks or nuns lived. Later, many of the monastic churches also became cathedrals.

Aisle A word coming from Latin meaning 'wing' – a passage each side of the nave.

Altar An elevated structure, or table, from which the sacrament (bread and wine) is served at the Eucharist (Holy Communion). The high altar is the heart of the cathedral and the focal point for its worship.

Ambos Twin pulpits.

Ambulatory A place for walking; a processional aisle usually around the east end behind the high altar.

Boss An ornamental carving at the intersection of a vaulted roof, sometimes also painted.

Capital A moulded or carved block on top of a pillar, sometimes richly ornamented.

Carrels Monks' study recesses.

Chancel The eastern end of the cathedral where the choir and high altar are situated, often separated from the nave by a screen. The word means 'an enclosure'.

Chantry A chapel, with a small altar, where masses were sung for the soul of a deceased person. These were suppressed at the Reformation.

Chapel A small place, with an altar, for private prayer or worship.

Chapter House A room for meetings of the Dean and Chapter – the clergy who are responsible for the cathedral, its fabric and services.

Charnel House A place where the bones of deceased persons were deposited.

Choir (or quire) The place where the singers and clergy sit, and where the daily worship is sung.

Choir aisle An aisle behind the area of the choir.

Choir screen A partition, often of carved lattice work, separating the choir from the main body of the cathedral.
Clerestory The upper part of the main wall, above the top of the aisled roof, with a row of windows.
Cloister The word comes from Latin, meaning an enclosed space. It is a covered walkway alongside the exterior walls of some cathedrals, usually those that were originally monastic churches. Cloisters served as a connection between the chapter house and other buildings, and provided a place where monks or nuns could work, have recreation and conversation. The cloisters had either an open colonnade or traceried windows, overlooking an enclosed cloistered garth (lawn).
Crossing The space formed at the intersection of nave and transepts.
Crypt A vaulted basement which, in earlier days, was used as a burial place beneath the chancel; the word means 'hidden'. Nowadays sometimes used for services.
Dorter Monks' dormitory.
Fan-vaulting Elaborate carved work in the form of fans, on ceilings.
Fluted Grooved.
Gable The triangular piece of wall at the end of a ridged roof.
Galilee Porch or chapel, usually at the west end. The name suggests a meeting place (see Mark 16.7).
Gothic Style of architecture, having high and sharply pointed arches.
Grisaille Painting in grey tints.
Lantern A structure on top of a tower or roof to give light to the building's interior, and as a crowning to the fabric.
Lady Chapel Usually built at the east end of the cathedral, behind the high altar, and dedicated to the Virgin Mary, who is sometimes called 'Our Lady'.
Lavatorium Monks' communal washing area.
Lierne vault Stone vaulting where the main ribs are joined, or tied as it were, by small ribs crossing from one to another.
Locutorium Place where rule of silence lifted for monks to speak together.
Misericord Bracket beneath a hinged seat in choir stalls; when seat tipped up support was given to a person standing during a lengthy service. Often grotesquely or humorously carved.
Narthex Large porch at west end of building.
Nave Main part of a cathedral where the congregation worships. The name comes from Latin *navis* meaning 'ship'; its shape resembles an upside-down ship.
Pectoral cross Small cross worn on the chest.
Pier A solid vertical mass of stone or brickwork for supporting an arch.
Pillar A slender upright structure, a column, usually circular, giving support to part of the building and capable of carrying a load.
Porphyry A rock through which crystals of a different colour are spread.
Refectory Monks' dining hall.
Reredorter Monks' lavatory block.
Reredos A screen or wall behind an altar.

Retrochoir The area behind the high altar, at the extreme east end.
Romanesque Architecture imitative of Roman, often called Norman, of the eleventh and twelfth centuries.
Rood The cross or crucifixion scene.
Rose window Circular window, usually resembling a rose. Often has the figure of Christ in majesty at centre, or of Virgin Mary, sometimes surrounded by apostles and other figures.
Sacristy A room for storing sacred vessels and clergy's vestments.
Sanctuary The part of the chancel in which the altar is set.
Sanctuary knocker Ornamental knocker on cathedral door which a fugitive could touch when claiming protection.
Screen A partition of stone, wood or metal separating parts of a cathedral; there is often a screen between the nave and choir.
Sgraffiti Impression on dark stucco by chipping away a picture on it in white.
Slype Passage leading out to monks' burial ground.
Tester Flat canopy over pulpit.
Tracery Ornamental stonework in a window.
Transept Transverse arms of a cathedral, running north and south. Usually referred to as 'north transept' or 'south transept'.
Triforium A gallery beneath the clerestory.
Triptych A set of three panels hinged side by side, and capable of being folded together, each panel is painted distinctively, as seen in an altar-piece.
Tuscan An order of architecture.
Vault Arched roof.

NOTES

PREFACE

1 Psalm 48.9.

CHAPTER 2

1 Psalm 136.1–3.
2 Daniel 2.47.
3 *The Oxford Companion to Music.* (Oxford University Press, Oxford, 1950.) p. 392.
4 Revelation 1.8.

CHAPTER 3

1 Revelation 22.2.
2 Hymn by J. S. B. Monsell (1811–75).
3 Exodus, Chapter 25 onward.
4 1 Kings 8.27.
5 Isaiah 52.10.

CHAPTER 4

1 Genesis 1.10, 12, 21, 25, 31.
2 Genesis 1.28.
3 Psalm 8.
4 'In Memoriam lvi', by Alfred, Lord Tennyson.
5 Genesis 9.3.
6 Hebrews 1.3.

CHAPTER 5

1 Genesis 22.9–14.
2 Genesis 23.
3 Exodus 2.
4 Exodus 17.8–13.
5 1 Samuel 17.
6 2 Samuel 18.33.
7 1 Kings 18.
8 1 Kings 19.3–9.

9 Psalm 23.
10 Psalm 103.13 and 14.
11 John 4.28.
12 John 4.14 (NEB).

CHAPTER 6

1 John 20.24–29.
2 Psalm 88.14.
3 Psalm 22.1; Matthew 27.46.
4 Psalm 13.
5 Psalm 39.12.
6 Psalm 40.1–3.
7 Psalm 10.13ff..
8 Psalm 33.12 and 13.
9 Psalm 148.
10 Luke 1.32.
11 Luke 2.19.
12 Hymn by W. Y. Fullerton (1857–1932).

CHAPTER 7

1 Song by David J. Evans.
2 Ecclesiastes 3.1.
3 Galatians 4.4.
4 Luke 9.51.
5 'I, the Lord of sea and sky', hymn by Daniel L. Schutte.
6 2 Corinthians 6.2.

CHAPTER 8

1 *Cathedral Meditations* by Joan Bristow.
2 Isaiah 31.5.
3 'Jesus, lover of my soul', by Paul Oakley (1997).

CHAPTER 9

1 Isaiah 6.2.
2 Matthew 1.21 and 23.
3 Luke 2.7.
4 Matthew 2.
5 Luke 2.41–52.
6 Luke 19.10.
7 'From heaven You came', by Graham Kendrick (1983).

CHAPTER 10

1 Psalm 98.7.
2 Isaiah 57.20 and 21.

3 Mark 1.16–20.
4 Luke 5.1–3.
5 Mark 1.29–31.
6 Matthew 14.22–33.
7 Mark 4.39 (AV).
8 John 21.15–17.
9 Isaiah 9.6.
10 Isaiah 58.1 (AV).
11 Isaiah 58.9 (AV).

CHAPTER 11

1 Isaiah 61.1.
2 Luke 7.22.
3 Mark 10.46–52.
4 Mark 7.31–37.
5 Mark 2.1–12.
6 Mark 5.25–34.
7 Mark 1.40–45.
8 Mark 5.1–20.
9 John 11.
10 Luke 18.18–29.
11 Isaiah 53.4 and 5.
12 Acts 12.
13 Acts 3.1–10.

CHAPTER 12

1 Luke 10.38–42.
2 John 4.
3 John 11.
4 Mark 5.25–34.
5 Luke 7.11–15.
6 Luke 13.10–17.
7 Luke 7.36–50.
8 John 8.3–11.
9 Luke 8.1–3.
10 Genesis 5.1 and 2.

CHAPTER 13

1 'The Crucifixion', cantata by J. Stainer, Matthew 26.40 (AV).
2 Luke 23.39–43 (AV).
3 Mark 15.39.
4 John 6.35.
5 John 15.1.
6 John 14.6.

CHAPTER 14

1 John 8.12.
2 John 1.4.
3 Hebrews 1.3.
4 Revelation 22.5.
5 Revelation 3.20.
6 'Some Reflections on the Background and Message of Holman Hunt's Picture' by Eric Hayden.
7 'Lord, the light of Your love', by Graham Kendrick (1987).
8 Matthew 16.18.
9 Matthew 5.14.

CHAPTER 15

1 2 Corinthians 5.10.
2 Matthew 24.36.
3 Matthew 25.31–46.
4 John 3.16 and 17.
5 John 3.18.

CHAPTER 16

1 Genesis 1, 2.
2 Isaiah 43.19.
3 Luke 1.35.
4 John 3.5 and 6.
5 Genesis 1.11.
6 Hebrews 1.3.

CHAPTER 17

1 Matthew 7.29.
2 Matthew 5.45.
3 Matthew 26.14–16.
4 John 13.30.
5 John, Chapters 14–16.
6 Luke 11.13.
7 Acts 1.8.
8 'There is a Redeemer', by Melody Green (1982).

CHAPTER 18

1 Acts 2.1–4.
2 Matthew 28.19 and 20.
3 Acts 1.8.
4 Psalm 123.2.

CHAPTER 19

1 Matthew 16.19.
2 Acts 2.36–38.
3 Luke 3.3.
4 Mark 1.15.
5 John 4.1 and 2.
6 Luke 22.54–62.
7 John 21.
8 Mark 1.40.

CHAPTER 20

1 Mark 1.35.
2 John 17.
3 Luke 22.39–44.
4 Romans 8.26.
5 Romans 8.27.
6 Mark 15.38.
7 John 17.22.

CHAPTER 21

1 Acts 10.15.
2 Acts 10.38.
3 Ephesians 4.2 and 3.
4 'O Spirit of the living God', hymn by James Montgomery (1771–1854).
5 Genesis 1.2.

CHAPTER 22

1 Luke 6.12–16.
2 Luke 22.39–44.
3 Matthew 6.25–34.
4 Mark 1.41.
5 Galatians 5.22 and 23.
6 Revelation 4.4.

The Society for Promoting Christian Knowledge (SPCK) was founded in 1698. Its mission statement is:

To promote Christian knowledge by

- **Communicating the Christian faith in its rich diversity;**
- **Helping people to understand the Christian faith and to develop their personal faith; and**
- **Equipping Christians for mission and ministry.**

SPCK Worldwide serves the Church through Christian literature and communication projects in over 100 countries, and provides books for those training for ministry in many parts of the developing world. This worldwide service depends upon the generosity of others and all gifts are spent wholly on ministry programmes, without deductions.

SPCK Bookshops support the life of the Christian community by making available a full range of Christian literature and other resources, providing support for those training for ministry, and assisting bookstalls and book agents throughout the UK.

SPCK Publishing produces Christian books and resources, covering a wide range of inspirational, pastoral, practical and academic subjects. Authors are drawn from many different Christian traditions, and publications aim to meet the needs of a wide variety of readers in the UK and throughout the world.

The Society does not necessarily endorse the individual views contained in its publications, but hopes they stimulate readers to think about and further develop their Christian faith.

For further information about the Society, visit our website at *www.spck.org.uk,* or write to:
SPCK, Holy Trinity Church, Marylebone Road,
London NW1 4DU, United Kingdom.